The Vigilant God

PETER LANG
New York • San Francisco • Bern • Baltimore
Frankfurt am Main • Berlin • Wien • Paris

Horton Davies

The Vigilant God

Providence in the Thought of Augustine, Aquinas, Calvin and Barth

PETER LANG
New York • San Francisco • Bern • Baltimore
Frankfurt am Main • Berlin • Wien • Paris

Library of Congress Cataloging-in-Publication Data

Davies, Horton.
The vigilant God : providence in the thought of Augustine, Aquinas, Calvin, and Barth / Horton Davies.
p. cm.
Includes bibliographical references and index.
1. Providence and government of God—History of doctrines.
2. Theodicy—History of doctrines. I. Title.
BT135.D29 1992 231'.5'09—dc20 92-13701
ISBN 0-8204-1496-4 CIP

Die Deutsche Bibliothek-CIP-Einheitsaufnahme

Davies, Horton:
The vigilant god : providence in the thought of Augustine, Aquinas, Calvin, and Barth / Horton Davies.—New York; Berlin; Bern; Frankfurt/M.; Paris; Wien; Lang, 1992
ISBN 0-8204-1496-4

The paper in this book meets the guidelines for permanence and durability of the Committee on Production Guidelines for Book Longevity of the Council on Library Resources.

Printed in the United States of America.

Contents

Acknowledgments

I wish to thank professor Daniel Hardy, Director of the Center of Theological Inquiry in Princeton, and my colleagues there over the past three years for their comradeship and encouragement, which means more than this formal expression of gratitude. Ad always, my wife, Marie-Hélène, has been my literary helpmate. I have also benefitted from the help of Michael Flamini, Senior Acquisitions Editor of Peter Lang, Inc.

Horton Davies, Princeton.
January, 1992

Introduction

If the road to Hell is paved with good intentions, then the road to Heaven is paved with failed theodicies discarded by faith. Milton even in the mid-seventeenth century felt able to "justify the ways of God to man" despite his suffering through blindness, while most recent theologians have abandoned the task, at least in the traditional terms advanced by Augustine, Aquinas and Calvin.

This book is an investigation of the strengths and weaknesses of the traditional defenses of the rule of God, views which many contemporary theologians have discarded too rapidly. The latter argue that it is not in natural theology amenable to reason, but in the revelation of God in Christ and in His Incarnation, Cross and Resurrection, that faith is warranted and sustained despite sin, suffering, doubt, and death. Anselm's conviction: *Credo ut intelligam* (I believe that I may understand) seems much more convincing in our day than the parading of five arguments for the existence of God, which Aquinas provided in his *Summa Theologiae* (itself an admirable rational and philosophical theology) which has not outlived its medieval usefulness, as the twentieth century Thomists have shown. These five "ways" (*quinque viae*) at best led to the conviction that it was reasonable to believe in the existence of God, but they said little positively about the nature of God whose existence they affirmed. However, in medieval civilization they corroborated the Biblical assertion "The fool hath said in his heart there is no God." This was good for the three monotheistic faiths of the Middle East and Europe–Judaism, Christianity and Islam. Moreover, Aquinas showed convincingly that the works of '*the* philosopher', Aristotle, many of whose writings were rediscovered in the thirteenth century, were not necessarily a menace to faith, but could be employed in Christian apologetical theology.

The difficulties of both a Platonic-Augustinian and an Aristotelian-Thomist doctrine of providence in our time have, however, forced many believers to become rigid fideists basing their conviction on the infallibility of Holy Writ, while others find the problem intellectually insoluble, but practically acceptable through faith.

John S. Whale, a Neo-Orthodox Congregationalist, in his book, *The Christian Answer to the Problem of Evil* says flatly: "... strictly speaking the problem is insoluble."[1] Albert Outler, a noted American Methodist theologian, outlines some of the difficulties in a doctrine of providence formulated on the old lines: "We can no longer argue for a doctrine that portrays providence as a divine genie, favoring the favored, or unrolling the script of history, with sneak previews as special service for the sharp-eyed and knowledgeable."[2] Even a Reformed theologian, proud of his Calvinist heritage, Theodore Plantinga, confesses: "I do not believe that those who seek a theodicy or a theoretical solution to the problem of evil will find it in Calvinism–or anywhere else for that matter ... . Thus Calvinism responds to the problem of evil with an eschatology rather than a theodicy."[3]

It will be observed that the appeal to eschatology is an appeal not to reason, but to special revelation based on the promises of life in the hereafter. The Anglican theologian Maurice Wiles, after asserting that the problem of evil is the Achilles heel of Christian theism, insists that the atrocities of the twentieth century have exacerbated the problem psychologically, if not theoretically, and asks: "Is it possible ... to do theology after Auschwitz and Hiroshima? And if it is, must not that theology eschew the task of theodicy altogether?"[4] The term 'theodicy' it should be recalled, etymologically means to affirm the righteousness of God, and it is used by thoughtful Christians who believe that they must affirm the inscrutability and mystery of God's ways. The French Reformed theologian Paul Ricoeur, referring to the Book of Job, which encourages accepting what cannot be understood, asserts that the death of providence must be accepted and hence "the path of theodicy has been closed off."[5] But even he, while denying that God controls every event, affirms a kind of theodicy in reference to the Christ of the Crucifixion who helps humans in their sufferings. Another French Reformed theologian, Jacques Ellul, in *Ce Que Je Crois*, a final summing up of his beliefs, denies that there is any systematic doctrine of providence in the Bible in a deterministic form, otherwise what is the point of praying in the Lord's Prayer, "Thy kingdom come, Thy will be done"? He insists that the word "providence" does not occur in the Bible, nor any equivalent, and that the conception of the divine control of every action in history is "inaccurate biblically and false theologically."[6] His objections to the traditional view of providence are two-fold: man would be turned into an automaton and God into a tyrant. The Lutheran theologian, Regin Prenter, believes that there is a mysterious unity between God's creative and redemptive will, but that this cannot be proved by reason. Indeed, when reason is used to try to demonstrate God's conservation, cooperation with and government of the world, it leads to the desperate conclusion that "providence is either responsible for all the evil and destructible elements of life, or evil is explained away as something non-essential." [7]

One is bound to ask why modern theologians find it almost impossible to affirm the Augustinian-Thomist-Calvinist view of the Divine control of events, which gave their exponents such comfort and support. While we shall in later chapters expound the traditional view in detail with the formidable defenses that Augustine, Aquinas and Calvin supply and the objections that they answer, it is worth considering the factors in the nineteenth century that have contributed to feeling its inadequacy. Langdon Gilkey has analyzed three major components of our modern secularism, which enable us to understand some of the major difficulties in the way of the modern mind accepting providence. With the growth of technology and urbanization humanity has become less dependent upon nature and its order. Increasingly, the "God of the gaps" disappears as technology seems to control the major areas of our life. Humans sense they have left God's world, where they shared in an eternal order, for a world where they have become the creators and determiners of a changing order. In the second place, this has also modified the views of human institutions and customs. Former authorities, previously unquestioned sources of divine order, are now powers with which one can negotiate. Finally, the world itself is desacralized. It is material and can be fashioned in virtually any shape we desire.[8]

Another clue to modern secularism is the recognition that three masters of modern thought have either ridiculed or otherwise minimized the role of God in the providential care of the world. Paley asserted the concept of design in the world, but Darwin denied it in the words: "There seems to be no more design in the variability of organic beings and in the action of natural selection than in the course which the wind blows."[9] Darwin said that a devil's chaplain could make a devastating case against a benevolent God in creation by stressing the clumsy, wasteful, blundering, low, and cruel works of nature. He concluded: "I cannot persuade myself that a beneficent and omnipotent God could have designedly created the Ichneumonidae with the express intention of their feeding within the living bodies of caterpillars or that a cat should play with mice."[10]

The two other thinkers who had a major impact on modern thought were Marx and Freud who followed Feuerbach and Nietzsche in considering religion as mere egoistic wish-projection. In 1844 Marx presented his doctoral dissertation to the University of Jena, titled, *Zur Kritik der Hegelsche Religionsphilosophie*, a critique of the philosophy of religion expounded by Hegel in which he concluded that religion was a fantasy created by man to make an unbearable life tolerable. Therefore, in his view it was "the opium of the people." It is significant that his prefatory motto to the dissertation was borrowed from Aeschylus and read: "In one word, I hate all gods." This illusion was evaluated by Marx as simultaneously a protest against oppression and an adaptation to it.[11]

Sigmund Freud, the father of psychoanalysis, also interpreted religion as an escape-mechanism from reality. His *Zukunft einer illusion* (1928), published in English as *The Future of an Illusion* claimed: "We tell ourselves that it is very beautiful indeed that there is a God, Creator of the world, a kind of Providence, a moral order, and a life hereafter—but it is very striking that all this is exactly as we would wish it ourselves."[12] When he returned to the subject of religion in his last major book, *Moses and Monotheism*, while he was prepared to admit that Western monotheism was an ascetic force supporting the renunciations necessary to make scientific endeavors possible, he also maintained that religion retarded the general acceptance of scientific discoveries. Ultimately he was a skeptic regarding dreams and myths as merely the subconscious projections of a group, which—for all their power on individuals accepting them—cannot be ontologically substantiated.[13]

Thus the major architects of modern thought shrink our traditional approaches to God's providential care for this world, for each considers theology to be only anthropology masquerading as transcendental, and man as a prisoner of a closed system in which human conflicts are explained without recourse to God.

The development of secularism is, of course, older than the last two centuries. As David Schuller recognizes, "The Renaissance, the Enlightenment, the Industrial Revolution, the Cybernetic Revolution—each marks a milestone on this path."[14] Each development made it increasingly difficult for the wayfaring man to take God, transcendent values, and holiness seriously.

In addition, our own century has witnessed an overwhelming series of dysteleological experiences, such as pogroms, concentration camps, famine, and horror of horrors—the Holocaust, that it might justly be termed the "Catastrophic Century." A conviction of the meaninglessness of life, its apparent lack of any purpose, and even its sheer absurdity, has been proclaimed by dramatists and novelists such as Ionesco, Camus, Kafka, Sartre, Simone de Beauvoir, O'Neill, Beckett, and others. Emile Caillet summed up the situation thus: "What used to be *The Pilgrim's Progress* has become *A Long Day's Journey into Night.*"[15] Moreover, the gigantic losses of life in World Wars I and II, the Armenian Massacre, the near elimination of Hiroshima and Nagasaki, and the endemic and continuing mass deaths from hunger in Africa, have created a mad and mournful world in our own time. No wonder that to many the correlation of a God of love with the murderous manifestation of evil appears to be only a futile whistling in the dark, merely wishful thinking.

Nonetheless, neither was Augustine's nor Aquinas's nor Calvin's nor is our own world an utopia. Augustine wrote *The*

City of God when the Roman empire was disintegrating under the attacks of the rampant, raging, raping, thieving Huns and Goths, while the desperately poor and frightened citizens were escaping to the shores of North Africa into Augustine's diocese of Hippo, and many Christians were blaming Christianity for the Fall of Rome and their troubles. His book was a superb attempt at justifying the ways of God to man, and he wrote a Christian philosophy of history precisely when the world around him was collapsing. We may note that according to J.N. Figgs, interpreting St. Augustine: "It is history as a whole, history from the creation of light until the Last Judgment, that is the Justification of God."[16]

Aquinas lived a calm life, but he wrote in a century when the Muslims were a continuing physical and mental threat to Christians, and when the greatest intellectual threat was the philosophy of Aristotle which denied the Christian doctrine of Creation by God *ex nihilo* (as described in Genesis) and affirmed a Deity without the compassion of the Heavenly Father taught in the Lord's Prayer, namely, the impassible "Unmoved Mover", and St. Thomas devoted his whole life to defending Christianity against the structurers of the immensely popular philosopher Aristotle and his Arabian interpreters. And Barth in our own day has had to fight secularism on all fronts with a Christocentric Deity, who is Triune. Calvin, whose theology had a deep affinity to Augustine, was a quiet French scholar, who was browbeaten into leading Geneva through the troubles of the Reformation, was always in the thick of controversy, and was forced to seek asylum for three years in Strasbourg, and whose only child died, knew the full meaning of adversity. Yet he wrote the finest Biblical systematic theology up to his day only perhaps to be equalled by Barth in our day. And Calvin's *Institutes* was itself, as also Barth's *Kirchliche Dogmatik*, a theodicy.

The aim of this book will be to review and to re-assess the Augustinian, Thomist, Calvinist and Barthian doctrines of providence in the light of their intentions, and in the perspective of the twentieth century interpretations of providence. We shall begin with a consideration of the Biblical doctrine of Providence, which all four theologians believed they were interpreting. All thought that God watched over his own, as Psalm 121 indicated: "Behold He who keeps Israel will neither slumber nor sleep." Hence, the title of this book, *The Vigilant God.*

Notes

1 Published by Abington Press, New York and Nashville, 1936, p. 13.

2 *Who trusts in God. Musings on the meaning of Providence* (New York: Oxford University Press, 1968), p. 70.

3 *Learning to live with evil* (Grand Rapids: Eerdmans, 1982), p. 135.

4 *God's action in the world.* The Bampton Lectures for 1986 (London: The S. C. M. Press, 1986), p. 39.

5 'Religion, Atheism and Faith' in *The Conflict of Interpretations* (Northwestern University Press, 1974), p. 455.

6 Paris: Grasset, 198, p. 208. The French original reads "Cette conception me semble inexacte bibliquement et fausse théologiquement." In the same paragraph the author adds: "Je crois qu'il n'y a pas de providence."

7 *Creation and Redemption* (Philadelphia: Fortress Press, 1967), p. 209.

8 *Naming the Whirlwind: The renewal of God-language* (Indianapolis: Bobbs-Merrill Co., 1969), pp. 36-38.

9 *Autobiography.* ed. N. Barlow (New York: Harcourt, Brace, 1959), p. 87.

10 Francis Darwin, *The Life and Letters of Charles Darwin* (New York: Appleton, 1898), II, p. 105, cited in ed. W. W. Wager, *European Intellectual History since Darwin* (New York: Harper, 1966), p. 22.

11 Ed. Mircea Eliade. *The Encyclopedia of Religion* (New York: Macmillan, 1987), 9, pp. 238b and 242b.

12 *Op. cit.*, p. 53.

13 *The Encyclopedia of Religion*, Vol. 5, pp. 435b and 437a.

14 "Sociology's reluctant participation in the dialog concerning Providence" in eds. Carl S. Meyer and Herbert L. Mayer, *The Caring God. Perspectives on Providence* (St. Louis: Concordia Publishing House, 1973), p. 14.

15 *The Recovery of Purpose* (New York: Harper & Bros., 1959), p. 20.

16 *Political Aspects of St. Augustine's City of God* (London: Longmans, Green and Co., 1928), p. 39.

Chapter 1

Biblical Sources for the Traditional Doctrine of Providence

Our investigation of the traditional doctrine of Providence in Augustine, Aquinas, Calvin and Barth requires us to list and analyze the Biblical sources of the doctrine, since the special revelation recorded in the Old and New Testaments is its prime source.

St. Augustine came to Christianity after spending nine years in the dualistic religion of Manichaeanism and subsequent time in Neo-Platonism. His is, therefore, a philosophical approach to theology, as is that of St. Thomas Aquinas, whereas Calvin's systematic theology and Barth's are consistently Biblical. Nonetheless, the Bishop of Hippo recognized the supreme authority of the Scriptures as the Word of God, and the absolute finality of the revelation of Christ, the Incarnate Word of God. He described the Christian's situation as follows:

> From the city [heaven] from which we are exiles letters have reached us; these are the Scriptures which exhort us to holy living. What do I say: letters? The King himself has descended in person. [1]

For Augustine the Scriptures are "holy, sacred, divine, infallible, inspired, the venerable pen of the Spirit." [2]

Like Aquinas and Calvin he devoted many years to the writing of commentaries on the Bible and in his diocese he preached a sermon daily, and often twice a day. His main exegetical works are commentaries on Genesis, the Psalms, the Harmony of the Gospels, the Gospel and the Epistles of John, Romans (unfinished), Galatians, and, curiously, no work on Ephesians, which clearly states the doctrine of predestination. Also, like Calvin in this, he insisted that it was the interior illumination of the Holy Spirit that led to the conviction of the salvific truth of Scripture. It is characteristic of him in his homilies in Hippo to appeal to the Divine Teacher, or His promised Holy Spirit, to reach the hearts of his hearers, as, for example: "May the Lord help me . . . Ask with me for success; your eyes for me, your heart for Him."[3] Maurice Pontet, expert on Augustine's exegesis, says that St. Augustine believed that in the act of faithful Biblical preaching the Holy Spirit slides into the soul, introducing the faithful to the interiority of truth, and by a mysterious empathy enabling them to taste the spiritual nature of God.[4] Further, Pontet maintains that Augustine averred that the vital breath of the same Spirit blew throughout the Psalms, the Gospel, and in the "divine sermon" expounding them. This is almost the exact equivalent of Calvin's doctrine of the *testimonium internum Spiritus Sancti* (the interior witness of the Holy Spirit).

Augustine, brilliant rhetorician that he was, yet lacked Calvin's command of both Hebrew and Greek. He appeared to lack Hebrew, and his Greek was competent rather than magisterial, so he was not as exact an interpreter of Scripture as Calvin was. His exegesis is often overly allegorical, yet always spiritual. Yet as Pontet concludes:

> He made a principle of only interpreting Biblical obscurities by illuminating them from other clearer passages. That is why he often finds himself reading into a verse what is not there, but he never finds there a truth which cannot be discovered elsewhere in the Bible. The local error yet remains a general truth, and confronted by such an exegesis the philologist is irritated, and the theologian reduced to silence. [5]

Peter Brown claims that Augustine has two motives for his preference for allegorical exegesis. One is that the sheer difficulty for the interpreter of Scripture makes the task more exhilarating. The other is that since the Fall human beings have no longer a direct awareness of God and have to use the awkward language of 'signs' for communication. [6]

John Calvin, both in training and linguistic competence, was a better exegete of the Scriptures than Augustine or Aquinas, and more consistent. He produced expository commentaries or homilies on almost the whole of the Bible, beginning with the Epistle of the Romans in 1540 and ending with Joshua in 1564.

He had an excellent command of Hebrew, Greek and Syriac, whereas Augustine knew only Greek and accepted the plenary inspiration of the Septuagint.

Some Calvin scholars claim that the Reformer believed in the verbal inerrancy of Scripture and point to a passage in the *Institutes*, namely IV, viii 9 in which Calvin calls the apostolic writers "sure and authentic amanuenses of the Holy Spirit" (*certi et authentici amanuenses* . . .). He certainly believed that the Scriptures taught inerrant doctrine, but he remarked on apostolic errors of translation from the Old Testament. Paul in Romans 3:4 is corrected by Calvin for mistranslating Psalm 51:4 and Luke is said to be in error in Acts 7:16, and he points out that Hebrews 2:7 renders the phrase in Psalm 8 incorrectly. On the Pauline error he observes:

> For we know that in repeating the words of Scripture the apostles were often frequently rather free (*in recitandis scripturae verbis saepe esse liberiores*) since they believed it sufficient if they cited them in accordance with the matter. For this reason they did not make the words a matter of conscience (*quare non tantum illis fuit verborum religio*). [7]

The ultimate authority of the doctrine in Scripture is the Holy Spirit, or the Spirit of Christ the Teacher promised to the disciples at Pentecost. Calvin insists vigorously:

> For as God alone is a fit witness of himself in his Word, so also the Word will not find acceptance in men's hearts before it is sealed by the inward testimony of the Spirit. The same Spirit, therefore, who has spoken through the mouths of the prophets must penetrate into our hearts to persuade us that they faithfully proclaimed what they had been divinely commanded.[8]

Not only so, but the Word and the Spirit belong inseparably together:

> For by a kind of mutual bond the Lord has joined together the certainty of his Word and of his Spirit so that the perfect religion of the Word may abide in our minds when the Spirit, who causes us to contemplate God's face, shines; and that we in turn may embrace the Spirit with no fear of being deceived when we recognize him in His Own image, namely, in the Word.[9]

Moreover, the very assent of faith is, according to Calvin, "more of the heart than of the brain (*l'assentiment est au coeur plutôt qu'au cerveau*) and of the disposition than of the intelligence" (*et d'affection plutôt que d'intelligence*). [10]

The radical change in the interpretation of Scripture at the coordinate time of the Renaissance and the Reformation was the new emphasis on the letter of the Bible, philologically determined, as contrasted with the medieval depreciation of the literal sense in favour of the three "spiritual" senses of Scripture, namely, the allegorical, the moral, and the analogical, which, while providing many original interpretations could also lead to some very dubious subjective ones. Henri Clavier rightly emphasizes Calvin's "respect for the letter [of Scripture], without servility, because it is the home of the Spirit."[11] For Calvin the exegesis of Scripture was the primary task of his life and Clavier does not exaggerate in claiming that "the *Institutes* are a prolonged commentary, as the *Ordonnances* [Ordinances for the religious life of Geneva] are an applied exegesis." [12]

Before looking at the uses made of the Bible by Augustine, Aquinas, Calvin and Barth, it will be necessary to examine the Biblical sources of the doctrine of Providence, which is our immediate concern in the ensuing pages.

The Scriptures generally indicate that God rules, directs and exercises his sovereign control over the world. This is indicated, in the first place, by the names of God. Yahweh is called the universal king. He is viewed as "the king of all the earth" who "reigns over the nations" (Psalm 47:7, 8). He is "king of the nations" (Jeremiah 10:7) as well as "the Lord of hosts" (Jeremiah 46:18, 48:15, and 51:57). This is also asserted in the New Testament for there God is described as "the great king" (Matthew 5:35), as "Lord of heaven and earth" (Matthew 11:25 and Acts 17:24). He is also "King of the ages" (I Timothy 1:17), "the blessed and only sovereign, the King of kings and Lord of lords" (I Timothy 6:15) and "the Lord our God, the almighty." (Revelation 19:6). But this King in the New Testament is the God and Father of Jesus Christ, who directs all things so that they shall be united in Jesus Christ: "things in heaven and things on earth." (Ephesians 1:10 and Romans 8:18-25 and 11:36).

The Bible also claims that God is director over the physical world, because "He changes times and seasons" (Daniel 2:21) and “He makes his sun to rise on the evil and the good and sends rain . . . ” (Matthew 5:45). God also “clothes the grass of the field . . . ” (Matthew 6:20) and “in his hand is the life of every living thing” (Job 12:10). “The young lions roar for their prey, seeking their food from God” (Psalm 104:21 and vv. 27, 30) and “the birds of the air . . . neither sow nor reap . . . and yet our heavenly Father feeds them” (Matthew 6:26) and “not one of them will fall to the ground without your Father’s will” (Matthew 10:29).

God also guides individuals. “I gird you though you do not know me” says God (Isaiah 45:5); “a man’s mind plans his way, but the Lord directs his steps” (Proverbs 16:9), and “my times are in thy hand” (Psalm 31:15), and it is God “who executes judgment, putting down one and lifting up another” (Psalm 75:7). According to Kittel, the clear sense of God’s providence or foreseeing and providing is found only once and that is in Job 10:12 in the words: “Thou hast granted me life and steadfast love; and thy care has preserved my spirit.”[13] Nevertheless, there are several other texts that imply the Divine guardianship, such as Psalm 145:20, “the Lord preserves all those who love him”, and Psalm 147:3 and 11: “He heals the broken-hearted and binds up their wounds” and “the Lord takes pleasure in those who love him, in those who hope in his steadfast love.”

According to Kittel, providence is found implicitly in the New Testament in a conviction that God’s will rules the world and achieves the goal of salvation,[14] “For from him and through him and to him are all things” (Romans 11:36; cf. also I Corinthians 15:28). The new understanding of providence comes, however, from Jesus with the recognition of his role in salvation. Paul, in particular, sees God’s love enacted in Christ and views his eternal redemption expressed in the golden chain of saving acts: “We know that in everything God works for good with those who love him, who are called according to his purpose. For those whom he foreknew he also predestined to be conformed to the image of his Son, in order that he might be the first-born among many brethren. And those whom he predestined he also called; and those whom he called he also justified; and those whom he justified he also glorified.” (Romans 8:28-30)

In addition to his control and direction of individuals, God also supervises the history of his own people, whether Israel or the New Israel, the Church. The supreme example in the Old Testament is, of course, the Exodus of the Israelites from Egypt by the crossing of the Red Sea, the giving of manna in the wilderness, and the arrival at Canaan, the promised land. This mighty act of God in redeeming Israel from Egyptian slavery is celebrated thus:

> "At the blast of thy nostrils the
> waters piled up,
> the floods stood up in a heap;
> the deeps congealed in the heart
> of the sea.
> The enemy said, 'I will pursue, I
> will overtake,
> I will divide the spoil, my desire
> shall have its full of them.
> I will draw my sword, my hand
> shall destroy them.'
> Thou didst blow thy wind,
> the sea covered them;
> they sank as lead in the mighty
> waters." (Exodus 15:9-10)

The New Testament equivalent for the Church is proclaimed by St. Paul: "No, in all things we are more than conquerors through Him who loved us. For I am sure that neither death, nor life, nor angels, nor principalities, nor things present, nor things to come, nor powers, nor height, nor depth, nor anything else in all creation, shall be able to separate us from the love of God in Christ Jesus our Lord." (Romans 8:37-39), and with the same assurance he insists: "for God is at work in you, both to will and to work for his good pleasure." (Philippians 2:13).

God also has a universal teleological control of the other nations of the earth. This is what Paul asserts in Chapters 9 through 11 in his Epistle to the Romans. St. Paul himself at the Areopagus in Athens declared: "The God who made the world and everything in it, being Lord of heaven and earth, does not live in shrines made by man, nor is he served by human hands, as though he needed anything, since he himself gives to all men life and breath and everything. And he made from one every nation of men to live on all the face of the earth, having determined allotted periods and the boundaries of their habitation . . . Yet he is not far from each one of us for 'In him we live and move and have our being'; as even some of your poets have said, 'For we are indeed his offspring.'" (Acts 17:24-28) One should also consider Paul's speech at Lystra (Acts 14:16 ff). God's ultimate goal is the establishment of His Kingdom, which will be consummated beyond history.

The Old Testament clearly indicates that Yahweh also shapes the destinies of other nations than Israel. The prophet Amos interprets God as saying: "Are you not like the Ethiopians to me, O people of Israel? . . . Did I not bring up Israel from the land of Egypt, and the Philistines from Caphtor, and the Syrians from Kir?" (Amos 9:7) Furthermore, God uses other nations to punish Israel for her infidelity: "Ah, Assyria the rod of my anger, the staff of my fury" (Isaiah 10:5). God can control priests, judges and even kings: "He leads counsellors away stripped, and judges he makes fools. He looses the bonds of kings and binds a waistcloth on their loins. He leads priests away stripped, and overthrows the mighty. He makes nations great, and he destroys them." (Job 12:17-19, 23) Daniel echoes the conviction of God's power over the nations: "His dominion is an everlasting dominion . . . he does according to his will in the host of heaven and among the inhabitants of the earth" (4:35); "he removes kings and sets up kings" (2:21) and "the Most High rules the kingdom of men and gives it to whom he will" (4:25). A foreign king, Cyrus, becomes the agent of Divine judgment: "Cyrus, whose right arm I have grasped, to subdue nations before him and ungird the loins of kings." (Isaiah 45:1) Jesus tells Pilate that he (Pilate) would have no power unless it had been given him from above (John 19:11); and "there is no authority except from God" (Romans 13:1). Moreover, God's ruling continues even in the eschatological age of the future as both Isaiah (9:7 and 11:6-9) and the Book of Revelation declare (19:6; 21:1-4, 22-27; and 22:1-5).

God even controls the supposedly free acts of humanity, so claimed Charles Hodge the theologian, but backing his assertion with the following series of Biblical citations: Proverbs 16:1 (cited earlier); "the king's heart is a stream of water in the hand of the Lord; he turns it wherever he will" (Proverbs 21:1); "Blessed be the Lord . . . who put such a thing as this into the heart of the king" (Ezra 7:37); "Incline thy heart to my testimonies" (Psalm 119:36). Hodge even claims that a large proportion of Scripture is based upon the assumption of God's "absolute control over the free acts of his creatures."[15] But here, as will be considered later, there is a paradox, if not a direct, flat contradiction in asserting simultaneously God's control and human free will.

It is also essential to recall that God's anger as well as his mercy in history is affirmed by the Bible. One of the most striking examples is the Divine degradation of King Nebuchadnezzar who is turned from a potentate into an animal that eats grass, as Daniel foretells the meaning of a dream the king had in which he saw a huge tree cut back to its roots, leaving only an ugly stump: "And as it was commanded to leave the stump of the roots of the tree, your kingdom shall be sure for you from the time that you know that Heaven rules." (Daniel 4:26) Yet before Nebuchadnezzar's degradation God told Jeremiah (27:3 ff) to inform five kings that God had given their lands to Nebuchadnezzar, king of Babylon. Also in Isaiah 5:12-13 it is recorded: "they do not regard the deeds of the Lord, or see the works of his hands. Therefore my people go into exile for want of knowledge."

God's continuing protection is affirmed in both Testaments. It is exhibited in the promises of God to Abraham that his posterity will be a vast multitude: "I will indeed bless you, and I will multiply your descendants as the stars of heaven and as the sand which is on the seashore," (Genesis 22:17, echoing what was previously announced in Genesis 13:16). It is made plain in the New Testament that this promise of protection does not only refer to the Jews as a separate people, but that Christians inherit the promises: "So you see that it is men of faith who are the sons of Abraham" and, again "And if you are Christ's, then you are Abraham's offspring, heirs according to promise." (Galatians 3:7, 29)

1. Two Apparent Conflicts

Our next concern will be to deal with two issues on which there are contradictions in Scripture. The first is the paradox, or at least great difficulty, of reconciling the Divine sovereignty and control of God with the moral necessity for freedom on the part of the human individual. The second is the contradiction between the Old Testament conviction of special Providence, and its apparent denial in the teaching of Jesus.

The paradox or contradiction of God's absolute control and human freedom is found in Paul's instruction to his converts in Philippians 2:12-13: "Therefore, my beloved, as you have always obeyed, so now, not only as in my presence but much more in my absence, work out your own salvation with fear and trembling; for it is God that is at work in you, both to will and to work for his good pleasure." If there were no free will, there would be no point in counselling or preaching, or even in reading the Scriptures. But, in fact, both Testaments are full of commands and instructions that presuppose the reality of human free will. The New Testament is filled with commands, which assume free will as much as the Decalogue in the Old Testament. Here are some leading Pauline examples: "Let each man take care how he builds upon it" (I Corinthians 3:10a); "But let each one test his own work . . . For each man will have to bear his own load" (Galatians 6:4); and "I appeal to you . . . that there be no dissensions among you" (I Corinthians 1:10); as well as, "But we exhort you brethren to do so more and more, to aspire to live quietly, to mind your own affairs, and to work with your hands, as we charged you" (I Thessalonians 4:11-12) and, finally, "As for you, always be steady, endure suffering, do the work of an evangelist, fulfill your ministry." (2 Timothy 4:5). James, too, appeals to his readers: "But be ye doers of the Word and not hearers only, deceiving yourselves." (1:22). Jesus also takes human responsibility for granted as reported in the Gospels. One example is: "Then Jesus told his disciples, 'If any man come after me, let him deny himself, take up his cross, and follow me.'" (Matthew 16:24). And, in the Sermon on the Mount, Jesus urged his hearers: "Let your light so shine before men that they may see your good works, and give glory to your Father who is in heaven." (Matthew 5:16).

One of the most interesting cases of the concurrence of Divine and human wills, and one in which God overrules an evil act for a good purpose, is that of Joseph and his brothers reported in Genesis 45:5-8 and 50:19 ff. His brothers had sold Joseph into the slavery of the Midianites but he ultimately became Pharaoh's right-hand man and finally was able not only to save Egypt from severe famine, but also to save his brothers as a 'remnant' and thus to fulfill God's promise to Abraham. Even when it is evident that God's sovereignty is seen in the event, the tension between God's sovereignty and man's responsibility still remains. The words of Joseph, "So it was not you who sent me here, but God", are hyperbolic, for Joseph does not condone the ugly fact of the action of the brothers, for in Genesis 50:19 he said to the brothers "As for you, you meant evil against me, but God meant it for good to bring it about that many people should be kept alive, as they are today." Thus the brothers cannot be treated as puppets, pulled by the strings of God. On the other hand, God is not pictured as deflecting the action of the brothers after the event and thus transforming it into an act of benevolence. As D. A. Carson comments: "Both God and the brothers entertain specific intentions in their respective roles in the same event; but their intentions are disjunctive."[16] Thus God works in deep hiddenness to use the worse things in human nature to further his plans to preserve human life. An even more striking example of the Divine overturning of human evil for the supreme good is, of course, the Crucifixion of Christ as the means of salvation.

Commenting on the Joseph story, G. C. Berkouwer writes: "The activity of God is revealed not as a *deus ex machina*, but *in* the action of the brothers. Their evil plan achieves historical realization, but the historical events are products of the Divine activity. God's good intents follow the mischievous path of the brothers, or, rather, the brothers unwittingly follow the path that God has blazed. They work in his service."[17]

Another acute conflict is involved in the doctrine of special Providence. It is clearly asserted in the conviction that God delivered Israel, his chosen people, in the great act of the Exodus and centuries later in bringing them back from exile.

On the other hand, it can be argued that the teaching of Jesus alerts his disciples to be aware of a simplistic equation of Divine protection for the good and Divine neglect for the evil. Reinhold Niebuhr, for example, insists that Christ's words discourage any belief in special Providence. Niebuhr remarks: "It is not true that God gives special favors . . . There is the vast dimension of nature where we cannot expect that God will put up a special umbrella for us against this or that possible disaster."[18] His conclusion is based on Luke 13:1-5: "There were some present at that very time who told him of the Galileans whose blood Pilate had mingled with their sacrifices. And he [Jesus] answered them, 'Do you think that these Galileans were worse sinners than all the other Galileans, because they suffered thus? I tell you, No; but unless you repent you will all likewise perish. Or those eighteen upon whom the tower in Siloam fell and killed them, do you think that they were worse offenders than all the others who dwelt in Jerusalem? I tell you, No; but unless you repent you will all likewise perish.'" Another event helps to confirm this denial of special Providence by Jesus. John 9:1-4 reports: "As he [Jesus] passed by, he saw a man blind from his birth. And his disciples asked him: "Rabbi, who sinned, this man or his parents, that he was born blind?" Jesus answered, "It was not that this man sinned, or his parents, but that the works of God might be made manifest in him. We must work the works of him who sent me while it is day, for the night cometh when no one can work." Niebuhr adds: "There is reward for goodness in life and there is punishment for evil, but not absolutely. The same law which punishes the criminal punishes the Savior. And there are three crosses: two for criminals who cannot meet the moral mediocrities of life, and one for the Savior who rises above it. This is life."[19]

There is another famous saying of Jesus which would seem to favor special Providence. This is Luke 12:6-7: "Are not five sparrows sold for two pennies? And not one of them is forgotten before God. Why, even the hairs of your head are all numbered. Fear not; you are of more value than many sparrows." Georgia Harkness[20] observes that this is an example of oriental hyperbole and is not to be taken seriously, especially if the two immediately preceding verses are recalled, which read:

"I tell you, my friends, do not fear those who kill the body, and after that have no more that they can do. But I will warn you whom to fear, fear him who, after he has killed, has the power to cast into hell; Yes, I tell you, fear him." Furthermore, if Luke 12:11 is taken seriously, it is clear that Jesus is both preparing the disciples for persecution and reassuring them at the same time: "And when they bring you before the synagogues and the rulers and the authorities do not be anxious how or what you are to answer or what you are to say; for the Holy Spirit will teach you in that hour what you are to say."

2. Predestination, Election, and Reprobation

Our final task in this chapter is to consider the Biblical bases of the correlated topics of Predestination, Election, and Reprobation, because they were central in the teaching of both Augustine and Calvin, and important also for Aquinas, and in their views they emphasized both the mercy and the sovereign justice of Almighty God in his providential order.

The sources of predestination in the New Testament are all Pauline with the possible exception of 1 Peter 1:20: "He was destined before the foundation of the world, but was made manifest at the end of the times for your sake." It is clearly expressed in Ephesians 1:3-5, 9-10: "Blessed be the God and Father of our Lord Jesus Christ, who has blessed us with every spiritual blessing in the heavenly places, even as he chose us in him before the foundation of the world, that we should be holy and blameless before him. He destined us in love to be his sons through Jesus Christ, according to the purpose of his will, to the praise of his glorious grace which he freely bestowed on us in the Beloved . . . For he has made known to us in all wisdom and insight the mystery of his will, according to his purpose which he set forth in Christ as a plan for the fullness of time, to unite all things in him, things in heaven and things on earth."

The essential point is that God determined who were to be his adopted children in Christ before the foundation of the world. The same conviction is expressed in Romans 8:28-29: "We know that in everything God works for good with those who love him, who are called according to his purpose. For those whom he foreknew he also predestined to be conformed to the image of his Son, in order that he might be the first-born among many brethren." The comfort that Paul gains from this doctrine is exultantly affirmed in verses 38 and 39 of the same chapter: "For I am sure that neither death, nor life, nor angels, nor principalities, nor things present, nor things to come, nor powers, nor height, nor depth, nor anything else in all creation, will be able to separate us from the love of God in Christ Jesus our Lord." The same conviction is echoed in 1 Thessalonians 5:9: "For God has not destined us for wrath, but to obtain salvation through our Lord Jesus Christ . . . "

It should also be added that Paul is so very anxious to insist upon the sheer generosity of the grace of Christ that he denies that any goodness on man's part will help to earn him salvation. Hence, God does not predestinate those whom he knows will be good individuals, and this he makes clear in retelling the story of Rebecca's two sons, Esau the elder and Jacob the younger, reporting "though they were not yet born and had done nothing either good or bad, in order that God's purpose of election might continue, not because of works but because of his call, she was told, 'The elder will serve the younger.' As it is written, 'Jacob I loved, but Esau I hated.'" (Romans 9:11-13). The final sentence, it should be noted, is a quotation from the prophet Malachi (1:2).

Paul asks whether there is injustice on God's part? And he answers: "He has mercy upon whomever he wills, and he hardens the heart of whomever he wills." Then the further objection is made that since God's will is irresistible, why should God still find fault? To which the flattening, if unconvincing response is made, "But who are you, a man, to answer back to God? Will what is molded say to its molder, 'Why have you made me thus?' Has the potter no right over the clay, to make out of the same lump one vessel for beauty, and another for menial use?" (Romans 9:20-22).

Paul records no further objection to this line of argument, but, in fact, one reply might have been made that the analogy is inaccurate: it is one thing to equate beauty with salvation, but damnation is surely minimized by calling the use of the pot menial? As we shall see later, both Augustine and Calvin cite the Potter image and the impossibility of man's finite mind comprehending the inscrutability and majesty of the hidden providence of God.

According to the doctrine of predestination there are two destinies determined before the creation of the world for human beings, for the elect eternal life, and for the reprobate only damnation. Hence we must seek the Biblical teaching first on Election. In the Old Testament Election is primarily that of the nation of Israel which is God's chosen people from the beginning. Later, however, because of its infidelities in worshipping strange gods and refusing to keep the Law, it is only a remnant that is called, because of its faithfulness, and this enjoys the New Covenant.

In the New Testament the thought of Election is developed fully in John's Gospel in terms of the calling of the disciples by Christ. After the exclusion of Judas, Jesus affirms, "You did not choose me, but I chose you and appointed you that you should go and bear fruit and that your fruit should abide; so that whatever you ask the Father in my name, he may give it to you." (John 15:16) Each reference to the election of the disciples is prefaced by solemn 'ego' declarations that He is the One who elects as in John 6:70; 13:18; 15:16, 19. In this case, as Kittel observes, "Hence election is not a secret counsel of God. It is enacted through the electing Son."[21]

In Paul and James it is not so much election of individual disciples from the world as it is the election of the community. Paul urges the Corinthian Christians to understand that since election is a demonstration of the sheer gratuitousness of God's grace, there is no reason for boasting on their part as the elect: "For consider your call, brethren; not many of you were wise according to worldly standards, not many were powerful, not many were of noble birth; but God chose what is foolish in the world to shame the wise, God chose what is weak in the world to shame the strong, God chose what is low and despised in the world, to bring to nothing things that are, so that no human being might boast in the presence of God." (I Corinthians 1:26-29). James 2:5 makes the same point as Paul in the course of criticizing discrimination between rich and poor in the Christian community, because by their election by God the poor become rich, thus emphasizing the triumph of Divine grace: "Listen, my beloved brethren, has not God chosen those who are poor in the world to be rich in faith and heirs of the kingdom which he promised to those who love him?"

The really distinctive New Testament emphasis in election is found strongly affirmed in the hymn of praise for all spiritual blessings that begins the Epistle to the Ephesians. According to Kittel, this is the single place in the New Testament where election is found with an express accent on eternity.[22] In view of the later theological development in Augustine, Aquinas and Calvin of the *decretum horribile* by which humans were destined for heaven or hell before the foundation of the world, it is important to see how little evidence there is in the New Testament for double predestination. We may well concur with Kittel: "It is unfortunate that the concept of election has been linked with the predestination controversy."[23] It is also worth observing that when Paul in Romans uses the analogy of the Divine choice of Jacob the younger, rejecting the elder brother Esau, and cites Malachi 1:3 ("Yet I have loved Jacob but I have hated Esau"), this was a choice of leadership, not a determination of salvation for Jacob and perdition for Esau. Carson, in discussing the doctrine of election in John's Gospel, concludes that, while men are regarded as responsible and not robots in their response to God, the result is: "The horribleness of the so-called *decretum horribile* largely disappears if men remain responsible for their sins and choices."[24] By emphasizing both Divine sovereignty and grace and human responsibility, John's Gospel provides both warning and comfort. It stresses final judgment at the end of history, the need for the obedience of faith, and the heinousness of rejecting Christ, and the eternal privilege of salvation as overwhelming compensation for the hostility of the world and its persecution. In the Old Testament this takes the form of "hardening". God is said to harden the heart of Pharaoh, as in Exodus 14:4, 10:20, 27, etc. God also frequently hardens the hearts of individuals in order to set them up for destruction, which is their just due according to the Biblical writers. All this is part of the general conviction that God is the sovereign disposer of all persons. It is equally clear that beings deserve condemnation for the evil they have practiced and hence the need for the Great Assize at the end of history where Christ will be the Judge.

A question still remains after considering predestination: How can God be just if he is controller of all individuals and before they are born chooses some for salvation and others for damnation? Can it be that God foresees the holy response of the good and saves them because of anticipated merits of theirs? This was the Armenian way of trying to save the justice of God, but it was rejected by Paul as well as by Augustine, Aquinas and Calvin. Their reply would have been that as all have sinned in Adam, all deserve perdition, so they should have no complaint, and God's generosity is seen in those who undeservedly have sinned but have been rescued by him. But this seems to smack of partiality in God. In any case, it becomes clear that although Jesus nowhere taught about the historical origin of sin, our theologians were immensely interested in the Adamic myth, which provided part of the Augustinian theodicy.

In the Book of Genesis there are, in fact, two accounts of the origin of evil. While Genesis 3:1-24 attributes it to Adam and Eve, Genesis 6 attributes its origin to lustful angels. Both accounts seek to clear God of any responsibility for evil, and to explain evil's universality in a world created by a God who is benevolent. Paul's use of the Genesis origins of evil is found in Romans, chapters 5 to 7, I Corinthians 15, and Galatians 5. He interprets the Adamic account as implying that Adam's sin communicates to posterity physical mortality, a condition of 'suppressed sinfulness' which knowledge of the Law stimulates into actual sinful acts, and the remedy for this condition is Baptism. Paul, however, does not write either of "Original Righteousness" or of "Original Sin." It is to Augustine (following Tertullian) that we must look to find the correlated concepts of "seminal identity" and "original sin" and the *massa peccati* and the inclusion of helpless infants in the *massa perditionis*. How far we have travelled from the teaching of Jesus which, while assuming the universality of sin, says nothing about its transmission by physical heredity or of its derivation from a primordial transgression.[25] How far we have travelled from Christ's assertion of the universality of human sin (as in Matthew 18:25, 5:19; 7:11; 12:23-24, and Luke 11:13), without any references either to any transmission by physical heredity or to any aboriginal transgression. The departures of Augustine, Aquinas and Calvin from the witness of the Bible in their use of the doctrine of predestination are a striking example of the need to correlate theology with Scripture.

Notes

1 Psalm 90, S. 2.1 and Psalm 103, S. 4.

2 *Confessions*, 7.21 and *Harmony of the Gospels*, 1, 35, 54.

3 S. 265, 9 and S. 291, 1.

4 *L'Exegèse de S. Augustin Prédicateur* (Aubier, 1947), pp. 38-9.

5 *Ibid.*, p. 585.

6 *Augustine of Hippo: A Biography* (Berkeley: University of California Press, 1966), pp. 260-261.

7 See John T. McNeill, "The Significance of the Word of God for Calvin", *Church History*, XXVIII (1959), pp. 140-145, and for a fuller account of the same topic, J. K. S. Reid, *The Authority of Scripture* (New York: Harper Bros., n.d.), Chapter II.

8 *Institutes*, I, vii, 4.

9 *Institutes*, I, ix, 3.

10 *Institutes*, III, ii, 9.

11 *Etudes sur le Calvinisme* (Paris: Librairie Fischbacher, 1936), p. 113.

12 *Ibid.*, p. 103.

13 *Theological Dictionary of the New Testament*, IV, 1013.

14 *Ibid.*, IV, 1016.

15 *Systematic Theology* (New York: Scribner's, 1872), I, p. 589.

16 *Divine Sovereignty and Human Responsibility, Biblical Perspectives in Tension* (Atlanta: John Knox Press, 1981), p. 10.

17 *The Providence of God* (Grand Rapids: Eerdmans, 1952), p. 100 f.

18 *Justice and Mercy*, ed. Ursula Niebuhr (New York: Harper & Row, 1974), p. 2.

19 *Ibid.*, p. 18.

20 *The Providence of God* (New York and Nashville: Abingdon Press, 1960), p. 24. Here she also remarks: "To read this passage in the mood of argument as to whether God keeps a ledger recording dead sparrows and hair follicles is to vitiate its meaning."

21 *Theological Dictionary of the New Testament*, IV, p. 172.

22 *Ibid.*, IV, p. 175.

23 *Ibid.*

24 *Divine Sovereignty and Human Responsibility*, p. 197.

25 N. P. Williams, *The Ideas of the Fall and of Original Sin* (London: Longmans, Green, 1928), pp. 32 ff. and 97 ff.

Chapter 2

St. Augustine's Doctrine of Providence

St. Augustine's thought develops from dualistic Manichaeanism through Neo-Platonic Idealism, to Christian theism. There are traces of all three in his subsequent thought. This is particularly the case in his interpretation of theodicy which exhibits not only traces of the philosophical positions he previously held, but also an extremism due to controversy, especially with the Pelagians. [1]

However much he was influenced by the philosophies of his time and by earlier theologians, his primary aim was to be a faithful expositor of the Christian oracles of Scripture which proclaimed the Word of God. Henri Marrou does not exaggerate in claiming that "For Augustine, Holy Scripture is the sum total of all truth, the source of all doctrine, the centre of all Christian culture, and of all spiritual life." He adds that careful scholars have counted in the edition of his complete works published by the Benedictines of St. Maur that there are 13,276 quotations from the Old Testament and 29,540 from the New Testament.[2] As a bishop it was his custom to expound the Bible once and sometimes twice daily, and always on Sundays, and over 500 sermons of Augustine survive, in addition to 113 books and 218 letters which frequently cite or recall biblical passages.

Admirable expositor as he was, we have already noted that he had no Hebrew. Furthermore, he read Greek "painfully" according to Eugène Portalie, who insists that the moral and political bent seen in his eloquence "led him to incontestable abuses in the mystical sense of Scripture." Portalie says further: "the two great qualities of his genius—the ardent passion of the African temperament and the prodigious subtlety of his spirit—

never left him the calm necessary for an exegete and resulted in violent or ingenious interpretations lacking solidity." [3]

For Augustine there were also two sources other than Scripture for the faith, even though Scripture's importance was absolutely primary. These two were Tradition and the Church. Tradition conveyed such apostolic desiderata as the baptism of infants, and offered guidance on the development of the Creeds as rules of faith. Further, the Church's authority[4] had to be respected because of the miracles effected at its birth, as well as for its holiness and its insistence upon unity. These factors had to be taken into account by the expositor of Scripture.

1. Augustine's View of Evil

The central problem inherent in all attempts at theodicy is to justify the goodness and almightiness of God in the face of evil, which seems to limit his benevolence or his supremacy.

Augustine's view of God as the supreme Good in a hierarchy of beings combined Neo-Platonism with the Trinitarian understanding derived from the Biblical revelation. He affirmed that all being is good–"a great good if it cannot be corrupted, a small good if it can."[5] For him evil was essentially non-being: "Evil is merely negative, the loss of good (*privatio boni*)."[6] This view he reaffirmed in the *Confessions*: "If things are deprived of all good, they cease to exist. So long as they are, they are good. Whatever is, is good. The evil then whose source I sought is not a substance, for were it a substance it would be good."[7]

This view of evil is connected with the conviction that God created the world out of nothing (*creatio ex nihilo*). Since God is omnipotent and supremely good, evil cannot be substantial or created, and human evil is explicable only as a voluntary turning away from good. Augustine maintains: "The cause of evil is the defection of the will of a being who is mutably good from the God who is immutable."[8]

It is difficult to find appropriate illustrations to make vivid the concept of evil as merely negative. Augustine himself suggested that evil might be thought of as a disease: "Take an animal's body, for example; its being diseased or wounded simply means its being deprived of health—after all, what we do when we provide a cure is not to make the evils in the body, its disease or wounds, go away and exist somewhere else, but to make them not to exist at all."[9] The logical difficulty here is that if you make something "not to exist" then it existed prior to your destruction of it, and hence evil has some sort of substance. Henri Marrou suggests that while in God there is all fullness, but that all other created things have a structure which might be called sponge-like, so that evil is a lack of being, "a hole, as it were, in the tissue of being." [10]

However vivid the illustrations may be, the argument for defining and defending the notion of evil as a negative is clearly unconvincing. John Hick repudiates the definition as totally inadequate to describe the damage caused by the malevolence of evil: "To describe . . . the dynamic malevolence behind the Nazi attempt to exterminate the European Jews as merely the absence of some good, is utterly insufficient."[11] Theodore Plantinga shrewdly saw that Augustine defined evil as negative in the context of ontology, while making it positive and real in the context of his ethics and theology, and in the latter respect falling in line with the Biblical conception of evil as moral sin.[12] On this more realistic view, moral evil is the consequence of the perverse and corrupt human will rebelling against God.

Before accepting the strength of the Biblical view of moral evil as sin, Augustine attempted another view of evil which has been described as the "esthetic" view. Essentially the point is made that evil is significant as providing a contrast with goodness to show the advantages of goodness in the universe. Augustine believed in the principle of plenitude in the universe, containing all possible varieties of creatures from the highest to the lowest, as being better than a universe containing only the highest type of being, a view derived from Plato's *Timaeus* and revived in Plotinus in the self-emanating One overflowing into all possible forms including the lower and dependent ones. Augustine, borrowing these views, insists that the order and transiency of nature provide the beauties of the reds and golds of decaying leaves in autumnal glory, but his esthetic view seems unable to include moral evil, although the Bishop of Hippo argues that sin, "the culpable misuse of freedom is not permitted to mar the perfection of God's universe, because the balance of the moral order is preserved by the infliction of appropriate punishment."[13]

Augustine's own defense was to urge, in the famous words, "God judged it better to bring good out of evil, than to suffer no evil to exist."[14] Ultimately, in Augustine's view, all varieties of creatures both high and low, angels, humans, and animals, as well as flowers, trees, and rocks, not forgetting the ugly as well as the beautiful, the perfect and the imperfect, sin and its punishment, form in the eyes of God a harmony which is good and admirable. Now God can undoubtedly bring good out of evil, as in the case of Joseph and his brothers selling him into slavery but in the Divine providence ultimately sustaining the entire family in a time of acute famine, and in the sublimest example of all turning the human viciousness of crucifixion into the Divine act of salvation.[15] However, according to Hick, the argument is vitiated since for Augustine the majority of humanity is eternally bound to sin and eternally to suffer the flames and tortures of Hell.

Here, again, ingenious illustrations make the esthetic argument for evil deceptively acceptable, whether evil is described as a contrast in mosaics which balance black and white tesserae, or we think of evil as the ugly knots on the underside of an exquisitely beautiful Persian rug. On these analogies evil is viewed as moral ugliness and is reduced to a mere contrast on the one hand, and on the other, to the underside and therefore not as visible and ugly as it is experienced in the moral life.

What, then, of the third Augustine argument that evil is no argument against God because it is entirely due to the human misuse of free will? Augustine, building his case upon the Book of Genesis believed that sin cannot be attributed to God the Creator because it arose from the sheer disobedience of Adam, and that original sin predisposed the entire issue of Adam and their progeny in all subsequent generations to sin.

2. Original Sin

The doctrine of Original Sin, in its Old Testament basis, its Pauline development, and Augustinian development in his Anti-

Pelagian writings, is not easily summarized or comprehended.[16] It is essential to understand at least its lineaments for two reasons. The first is that this is the basis of Augustine's blaming of man for sin, and acquitting God of any part in its origin or spread. The second reason is that it is also the basis of his defense of the doctrine of Predestination, another essential part of his doctrine of Providence.

As Gerard Bonner[17] points out, the doctrine is itself partly based on the Latin translation of Romans 5:12, which reads: *Propterea sicut per unum hominen in hunc mundum peccatum intravit, et per peccatum mors, et ita in omnes homines mors transivit, in quo omnes peccaverunt.* 'Therefore, just as sin entered this world by one man and through sin, death; so death passed in to all men, in whom all sinned.' The critical words are the final four of the citation: *in quo omnes peccaverunt*–'[in Adam] all men sinned.'

The Greek text reads ἐφ᾽ ᾧ πάντεζ ἥμαρτον and the Revised Standard Version translates the four final words as "because all men sinned." It is probable that Augustine derived the idea that all humans existed potentially in the seed of Adam from Ambrosiaster, a fourth century popular Roman commentator on Romans, for he had interpreted the *in quo omnes peccaverunt* as referring to Adam, adding: "It is clear that all have sinned in Adam as in a lump (*quasi in massa*); for since he was corrupted by sin, all whom he begot have been born under sin."[18] Augustine, however, went beyond Ambrosiaster in his interpretation of seminal identity's consequence in that he regarded original sin as original guilt, using the juridical term *originalis reatus*[19] as its definition. Further, this guilt is linked with a vice (*vitium*) or disease which determines the manner in which we inherit Adam's guilt and which dominates our lives. This is concupiscence or lust.

Before the Fall Adam was thought to enjoy in Paradise perfect health and freedom from concupiscence, with the result that his will and his reason were in complete control of his body's actions. But all this was dependent upon Adam's obedience to God, so that his contumacious disobedience to God caused him to lose control of both reason and will. This is clearly seen in his sexuality and the shame that it brought to both Adam and Eve on discovering their nakedness. For Augustine this disobedience of the will is caused by human appetites, the chief of which is sexual desire, concupiscence, which is involved in the very act of perpetuating humanity. He writes:

> Although therefore there are many lusts, yet when the word lust is spoken without any mention of the object, we commonly understand by it sexual desire by which the generative parts are excited. For this holds sway not only in the whole body, nor externally, but also dominates within, moving the whole man with such a mixture of sexual emotion and carnal appetite that the bodily pleasure so produced is the highest of them all, so that in the moment of consummation it overwhelms almost all the light and power of cogitation.[20]

It is this powerful concupiscence which conveys the guilt of original sin from parent to child in the act of generation. While the sickness is cleansed in Baptism, its effects are not overcome.[21]

As a result all born by human generation are a mass of sin, lust, and perdition, justly deserving to be damned, even if they commit no actual sins, unless they are purified by the water of Baptism. Even unbaptized infants are also damned, although such incur a milder penalty; *In illa damnatione minima non tamen nulla,* and the penalty is required because they inherit original guilt.[22]

It is Christ alone, God the Son Incarnate, true God and true man,[23] by whom the elect are freed from original sin and guilt, because He was born of the Virgin Mary, who was completely pure, overshadowed by the Holy Spirit, and because He offered on the Cross a spotless and acceptable expiatory sacrifice for the sins of the world. His death was the ransom paid to deliver the elect from the powers of death, the Devil and Hell.[24]

3. Predestination

Here we must introduce the doctrine of Predestination, based on the eternal Divine decree, which limited the extent of salvation, preventing it from becoming universalistic as in Origin. This doctrine–a "giddy" one, according to Peter Brown[25]–is expressed most clearly in Epistle 186, especially in section 7, where Augustine offers his own summation of the doctrine with its Pauline foundations:

> So then, God has certain and definite foreknowledge of the total number of the saints, for whom in their love of God, which he has bestowed on them through the Holy Ghost poured out in their hearts (Rom. 5:5), 'all things work together for good, for those who have been called according to his purpose. For those he foreknew he also predestined to be conformed to the image of his Son, in order that he might be the firstborn among many brothers. But those he predestined he also called'—here we must supply 'according to his purpose'; you see, there are others too who are called, but not chosen (Matt. 20:16), and therefore, not called according to his purpose. 'Those whom he called'—according to his purpose—'he also justified, and those he justified he also glorified' (Rom. 8:28). These are the sons of promise, these are the chosen ones, saved by grace's choice, as it says, 'if by grace, not now by deeds; otherwise grace is no longer grace' (Rom. 11:6). These are the vessels of mercy, in which God makes known the riches of his glory, even through the vessels of wrath (Rom. 9:23). These achieve through the Holy Ghost one heart and one soul (Acts 4:32), which blesses God and does not forget the benefits of him who is gracious to its iniquities, who redeems its life from corruption, who crowns it in mercy (Ps. 102:2). For it does not depend on him that wills or on him that runs, but on God showing mercy (Rom. 9:16).
>
> The rest of mankind do not belong to this company, though their souls and bodies, indeed their whole nature, apart from the flaw introduced into it by a proud and headstrong will, are the work of God's goodness. The reason God in his foreknowledge created them was to show just what free will, when it goes its own way, is worth without his grace; and also, by contrast with their justly deserved punishments, to teach the vessels of mercy the value of what has been conferred on them, seeing that it is by no distinction or merit of their own achieving they have been picked out of the bunch, but only by the gratuitous grace and free favour of God. In this way might every mouth be stopped, and he that boasts, boast only in the Lord (I Cor. 1:31).

Thus God has from eternity separated humanity to exhibit His mercy in some, the elect, and in others, the reprobate, the vengeance of His divine justice. Augustine's defense for this double Predestination is that if all were damned, He could not exhibit His mercy, and if all were to be saved, He could not exhibit His justice.[26] It only needs to be added that the number of the lost exceeds that of the saved, so that the elect have the more reason to praise God for His mercy in freeing them from a just condemnation.[27] Finally, avers Augustine, there should be no complaint because the reprobate deserve their deserts, and the elect are joyful in their gratitude for the exhibition of Divine mercy.[28] Even in the case of twins, if one is saved and the other damned, Augustine can only conclude that God's will is inscrutable on earth, but will be unveiled in eternity: "Two little children are born. If you ask me what is due, they both cleave to the lump of perdition. But why does its mother carry one to grace, while the other is suffocated by its mother in its sleep? . . . Both have deserved nothing of good, *but the potter hath power over the clay, of the same lump to make one vessel unto honour, and another unto dishonour.*"[29]

The only efficacious antidote to universal sin is grace, and Augustine is rightly renowned as the "Doctor of Grace". He envisages grace as having two important functions: to provide forgiveness for original and actual sins, and also (and this is his significant addition to the theology of St. Paul) to reimpower the weakened will to make it capable of the obedience of faith. St. Paul claimed that justification by faith was the heart of the Gospel, requiring a conviction in the heart that Christ was the Saviour, independent of any human merits, but for Augustine there was a legal element in his understanding. He interpreted *justificare* as *justum facere: Quid alium est enim, justificati, quam justi facti; ab illo scilicet, qui justificat impium.*[30] Augustine's chief stress was on the reinvigorating of the will, rather than on absolution which was secondary.

Just as the first Adam ruined the race, the second Adam, Christ, is the Savior of humanity. As it was the *vitium* of *concupiscentia* that was the cause of humanity's downfall, the cause of its salvation is *caritas*, that love which renews the will by infusion and is the gift of the Holy Spirit. Christ was made sinful that sinners might be treated as righteous:

> Christ was made sin, that we might become righteousness, not our own by God's, nor yet in ourselves but in Himself . . . just as He Himself showed by the likeness of the sinful flesh, in which He was crucified, that the sin was not His own but ours; . . . so that because there was no sin in Him, He might in a way die to sin, while dying to the flesh in which there was a likeness to sin, and since He Himself had never lived accord-

ing to the old sinful nature, He might signify by His resurrection our new life renewing itself from the ancient death, by which we were dead in sin.[31]

The parallelism is perfect and the God-man who was conceived without concupiscence,[32] preserving Him from all faults, is therefore an exemplar of perfect holiness and perfect love, but He has all the other vulnerabilities and weaknesses of human nature so that He understands the human lot. The work of Christ is two-fold: He is able to appease God on behalf of and in the name of humanity, and He is able to convert the heart and will of humanity on God's part.

4. Two Views on Grace and Freewill

Augustine stresses that man has free will and is not an automation or a puppet whose strings are pulled by God, and that he has the power to choose between alternatives. This viewpoint was consistently maintained in the early work, *De libero arbitrio*, as in the *De Civitate Dei*, a work that was written and published much later. However, Augustine insisted that in one essential area man does not have freedom: he cannot choose God and live for Him instead of for himself without Divine help, and that help is Grace. Moreover, grace involves not only God's revelation of Himself, but also the persuasion of the will to enable man to turn from self to God. Augustine the rhetorician masks this limitation in freedom by arguing that true freedom is slavery to God, and that freedom to disobey God is the vilest servitude of all, but these paradoxes do not finally hide the serious diminution of human liberty.

Augustine expounded two different views of grace, one early and another late. At first he believed that grace is given to those who have faith. Later, however, he insisted that faith itself is a divine gift, and that no one can believe and trust unless so moved by grace, which is given by God regardless of human merit whether actual or foreseen. Augustine affirms: "He [God] goes before the unwilling that he may will; He follows the willing that he may not will in vain."[33] And Augustine sums up his view in the famous words that became a red flag to the theological bull Pelagius: "Give what You command, and command what You will."[34]

In all of this Augustine had the laudable desire to show the total dominance of grace in God towards the wholly undeserving, and thus to exclude all human merit or boasting, as St. Paul had done. But if, as we have seen, this was all effected by a Divine decree in eternity before the world was created or any human being, then at the crucial point of faith–man's response to God–human responsibility is greatly reduced, if not fully negated, and the love of God is turned into irresistible grace,[35] that is, sheer power. Furthermore, if God is absolute controlling Will, it is logically difficult not to make Him ultimately responsible for evil. "It is not to be doubted", wrote Augustine, "that the will of God who made all things that He would in heaven and earth, and who also made those things which are to come, cannot be resisted by human wills so that He may not do what He will."[36] Yet in another statement Augustine, fearful that his virtual denial of human volition will logically force him to admit God's responsibility for sin, affirms human willing: "Otherwise, if there be no volition from Him, God is the author of sins, which God forbid!"[37] Clearly, there is a serious inconsistency here.

Augustine's reduction of human responsibility however unintended is further seen in his view that the perseverance of the elect is entirely the gift of God's grace to enable them to persevere until the end. His late books on *The Predestination of the Saints* and *On the Gift of Perseverance* were written when the hordes of the Vandals were approaching the coast of North Africa from Spain, and the bishops had good reason to fear their flocks would renounce the Christian allegiance under torture and persecution. Not surprisingly, Augustine held that perseverance in such circumstances was the supreme gift of God for by it God would grant His own immovable stability. Predestination might seem irrelevant to monks cooperating with God in their salvation in the comparative safety of Marseilles, but, as Peter Brown rightly insists, for Augustine, anticipating crisis, "it was a doctrine of survival, a fierce insistence that God alone could provide men with an irreducible core."[38]

5. Evaluation

From exposition we proceed to evaluation, meaning by that both the strengths and weaknesses of St. Augustine's theodicy.

The primary strength of his exposition is his dazzling sense of God's care and protection of the universe which His imagination has fashioned in beauty and goodness, with infinite inventiveness, and, in particular, His protective love for those whom He has adopted in Christ. The power and mercy of God are the central emphases of his theology, which revere God as Almighty and Heavenly Father. He never impugns God's love and justice, and is quick to attack those like Pelagius or Julian of Eclanum, who appear to do so. He will never allow human beings to boast of their virtue, but insists that they remain humble and awed by the Divine majesty.

Another quality of Augustine is his subtle exploration of the human psyche, admiring the coolness and balance of reason, and its almost insatiable curiosity in seeking the origins and causes of all things (such as only an able philosopher could appreciate). Equally, he is fascinated and disturbed by the splintering and shattering of cogitation by the emotions, especially by concupiscence. He is acutely aware of the deceptions and illusions of sin, its excuses and defenses and idolatries that it maintains in the ever volatile human heart.

Moreover, Augustine is the first to demonstrate that God's grace finds its most powerful effect in making the will consent, contrary to the thrust of original sin, to accept the obedience of faith. Augustine insists that God works on our wills outwardly in the preaching of the Gospel, but inwardly in our souls, since no one is master of his first thoughts. No one who has ever read through *The Confessions*, that earliest example of the soul laid bare before the holy scrutiny of God with the honesty of the future saint, will wish to deny that Augustine is a master psychologist.

Nor can it be denied that he is also an admirable expositor of Holy Scripture, except when the penchant for allegorical and subjective interpretations takes over. In at least two cases, he seriously misinterpreted St. Paul. As we have seen earlier, his reading of Romans 5:12 made the doctrine of original sin blacker than the Book of Genesis or the Epistles of St. Paul.

Similarly, he misinterpreted the clearly universalistic meaning of Paul's saying, that "God wills all men to be saved."[39] He qualifies the plain sense by restricting its application to 'many' or to 'the predestined' or 'from every race and class'.[40] Yet, despite these and other errors, Anne Marie LaBonnardière rightly insists that Augustine is a Biblical theologian par excellence, since his teaching springs directly from Scripture, and she warns that "to the degree one disregards this primordial fact in the study of St. Augustine's works, one is deprived of the illumination of the scientific value which every well-attested fact can possess, but above all this furnishes the best means for comprehending the Augustine *oeuvre.*"[41] He had the profoundest respect for the Divine wisdom of the Scriptures. After he had completed his huge commentary on the Book of Genesis and had searched widely in the Bible for the opening chapters of his *De Trinitate*, he reported from experience: "For such is the depth of the Christian Scriptures, that even if I were attempting to study them and nothing else, from boyhood to decrepit old age, with the utmost leisure, the most unwearied zeal, and with talents greater than I possess, I would still be making progress in discovering their treasures."[42]

As his great work *The City of God* demonstrates, Augustine was one of the first philosophers of history, and his tracing of the providential rule of God in the world must have owed much to the Hebrew and Christian conception of a Divine covenant between God and humanity. He, further than any Christian before him, sees God as the Lord of history, rejecting all the alternative views of his times which accounted for historical events on the grounds of fortune, fate, or the stars, or the Stoicism which in its determinism utterly denied a role for the human will. He is unwilling for such alternative views to eliminate the role of the Divine will in its providential guidance of both individuals and political societies, as he explains in Book V. In magisterial fashion in Books XI and XXII Augustine traces the origins, developments, and final ends of the two cities, or societies, the eternal one being the City of God, and the temporal one the City of Man, the first being the community of the elect, and the second being the society of those who aspire to the honor, power and glory of man. He even considers the beneficial role of Christian emperors, providing a model which Charlemagne was to use four centuries later as Holy Roman Emperor.

Further, as Bishop of Hippo, head of a combined ecclesiastical court and spiritual clinic, offering moral and spiritual judgments and counsel, and almost daily applying Scriptural wisdom in his homilies delivered to a large and varied congregation, he was an exemplary pastor, rigorous with the proud, gentle with the timid, and always the compassionate interpreter of the *caritas Dei*. It is only in some of his most bitter polemics with the Donatists or the Pelagians that he lost the charity he exemplified in his own diocese so magnificently in sermons.

Besides, in all his writings, polemical or non-polemical, doctrinal, expositions of the Bible, or epistolary, he was the consummate rhetorician, whose imagination was a veritable factory for making images and analogies, inventing memorable and pithy phrases famous for their assonance and balance, clear when very complex in thought, and eminently quotable. He was a master at the art of persuasion by appealing to both dialectics and the emotions.

And all these gifts were used to the greater glory of God so that Augustine became the greatest theological teacher of Western Christendom, exactly when he was needed most, at the breakdown of the Roman Empire, and his doctrine still has its ardent defenders, to say nothing of its profound impact on theologians or religious philosophers as different as Aquinas, Luther, Calvin, Bossuet, Pascal and Kierkegaard.

But not even Augustine was an uncracked mirror reflecting the Divine revelation. Despite his splendid achievements and profound influence, his theological system has not gone without criticisms, and to these we now turn. Without doubt Augustine was genuinely horrified by sin, and especially by lust, the sin that had controlled his life until his conversion. It seemed to him that this alienation from God was like the pollution of adultery. This was the primal, original sin of Adam, the result of concupiscence that carried the desperate sentence of death and damnation for all of Adam's progeny. What made it so fiendish was that the very process of generation demanded the gratification of sexual desire, and is therefore at the same time an extension of concupiscence and a penalty for it. In this regard Augustine can be accused of making his autobiography also everyman's biography.

Furthermore, it seems that he had no sense at all of sexual intercourse as a deep expression of marital affection. G. W. H. Lampe observes that for Augustine "unless sexual intercourse within marriage is directed towards procreation it is a form of prostitution: the wife is then joined to a man for the purpose of gratifying his lust in return for certain benefits."[43] Moreover, it can be argued more compellingly that rather than concupiscence, it is pride that leads to the rebellion of sin, that is the desire "to be as gods" (Genesis 3:5), acknowledging no superior. That is the ultimate treason of disobedience to the only true God. In addition, it is a legal fiction to condemn the children of guilty parents for the sins of their parents. Moreover, as Gerard Bonner rightly remarks: "His Theory of Original Sin, though ingenious, is too much based upon a faulty physiological theory [seminal identity] and an untenable conception of responsibility to be acceptable today . . . "[44] Nor, since Darwin, can moderns accept a view of primitive man as more advanced rationally and morally such as the Adamic mythos asserts, however valid the moral and religious lessons it means to inculcate.

A second major criticism of Augustine must be made. That is, admirable as he is as the strongest exponent of Divine Grace, he often falls into legalism that overshadows the predominant mercy of God. One example previously referred to is his idea of seminal identity which treats original sin juridically. The same legalistic rigidity is seen in his insistence that unbaptized infants are doomed to Hell without exception. To cite Bonner again: "It is not merely the fashion in which Augustine consigns unbaptized infants to eternal pain which repels us . . . As terrifying is the detachment with which he contemplates the damnation of the greater part of the human race, among whom there are many who are lost because time or space or their condition of life prevented them from having the Gospel preached to them."[45] Augustine does not speak, as Calvin will later, of the *decretum horribile* (terrifying decree) of Double Predestination; but he is perfectly willing to assert that God is just to condemn the majority of humankind to damnation, without observing that God's gratuitous mercy to the elect can just as easily be interpreted as Divine capriciousness and the rankest favoritism, since it is God who gives the grace of salvation, irrespective of merit, to some but not to others. Hence, in this doctrine in particular, we are more aware of the absolute *power* of God than we are of the Divine love which seeks out the lost, the least, and the last, as coruscatingly visible in Christ's Incarnation and Death on the Cross in which He cried "Father, forgive them, for they know not what they do . . . "[46]

A great and original mind such as Augustine's was, must occasionally produce inconsistencies, and he did exactly that. Odilo Rottmanner, in a profound analysis of his doctrine of Predestination, discovered a serious disaccord between Augustine's theological theory and his practical advice. The gentleness of his personal counselling is unchanging, but, in contrast, his theory developed increasing rigor until it virtually abolished human freedom in relation to God. The destruction of human free will was effected by the doctrine of irresistible grace.[47] It is interesting that before 397 Augustine had been willing to admit that while the call to faith was the result of Divine grace, its acceptance was the fruit of human free will. In the *De spiritu et littera* while affirming that God operates on the will of man even for faith, and that it is always God's mercy which goes before us, yet Augustine insists "but to respond to the Divine calling as well as to refuse it, that, as I have said, belongs to the will."[48] It was while he was deeply involved in rebutting the views of Pelagius and his brilliant defender, Julian of Eclanum, that Augustine gave more to Divine grace and less to human liberty, until he finally asserted that the liberty of the will could only decide against God, and was therefore ultimately slavery not liberty. Thus, he appears to assert liberty, when in fact he is paradoxically defining free will not as freedom from restraint, but as freedom from evil: "For it was expedient that man should be at first so made as to be able to will both good and evil, not without reward if he willed good, nor without punishment if he willed evil. But in the future life it will not be in his power to will evil. However, he will not be deprived of free will. On the contrary, his will will be all the freer when it cannot be the slave of sin."[49] Here one senses that the brilliant rhetorician has practiced sleight of hand on us. The result is that the ordinary sense of moral liberty is lost in his theological writings, however much it was affirmed in his personal advice in the homiletical task.

As an example of the gentler Augustine consider the following excerpt from Sermon 344.4: The blood of the Lord if you so wish is given for you, if you will not wish it, it is not given for you. (*Sanguis Domini, si vis, datus est pro te, si nolueris esse, non est datus pro te.*) Henri Rondet explains this contradiction in Augustine thus: "A prisoner of too anthropomorphic an idea of the gratuity of the Divine gifts, Augustine could not conceive that grace could be gratuitous if it is offered to all."[50] Here again the legalism of Augustine reappears. When he is asked why all do not receive grace, he replies it is because God is a Judge.[51]

There are inexplicable and unjustifiable elements also in the theodicy of Augustine. He maintains that all the evil in the world is due "either to sin or the punishment for sin"[52]—a view which is rejected by the Book of Job and by Christ Himself in Luke 13:1-5 and John 9:1-5. There is also a contradiction involved in affirming that an unqualifiedly good Adam sinned, since, as John Hick argues, this is to say that he was not good in the first place and God therefore created him imperfect from the beginning.[53] Following Hick's lead William Willimon insists that "by putting all the blame on the shoulders of humanity, human choice of evil is rendered unintelligible. What on earth would lead perfect people to destroy their idyllic bliss through their rebellion?"[54] Augustine had an excellent insight in believing that sin that led to redemption was much better than sheer innocence that left room for neither. He insisted, as cited earlier, that "God judged it better to bring good out of evil than to allow no evil to exist."[55] The snag in Augustine's theodicy is that his insight is effectively destroyed by the assertion that the majority of humanity will not benefit by it, since they are doomed to everlasting punishment.

We may conclude our chapter by reminding ourselves of Augustine's great defense of God's goodness, supreme power, and grace, and of this theologian's horror of sin and heresy, and his admiration of holiness. But we cannot forget his impersonal view of sin as either absence of good or sheer sexuality, his subpersonal view of the perfection of the world as requiring imperfection as a contrast by which to create aesthetic harmony, his legalism, his conception of grace as power rather than graciousness which invites rather than dominates, and most serious of all, the failure to insist on the personal rather than the substantial in the relationships of God to humanity. (The latter may be more appropriate for God's relationship to the natural world), for the personal element is obligatory in any theology founded upon God's self-disclosure in the Incarnation where the Divine love is expressed in Christ as One who teaches, heals, forgives, challenges, and reconciles, all radically personal relationships. [56]

Ultimately, for Christians, at the deepest level, the mystical sense of unity with Christ in His sufferings and His consolations, as part of the Body of Christ, creates inner peace as well as hope and love. Augustine expressed this vividly in his commentary on the Sixty-second Psalm: "If He is the Head, we are the members. The whole of His Church wherever she is scattered constitutes His body of which He is the Head. We mean not only the faithful now living, but also those who existed before us, and those who will succeed us to the end of time; all these do indeed form part of His body. He who is ascended into Heaven is the Head of this body (Colossians 1:18) . . . For whatever He has suffered with Him, and what we suffer He too suffers with us . . . Whatever His Church suffers by way of this life's tribulations, temptations, constrictions and deprivations (for she must be schooled to be purified in the fire) this He also suffers." This fellowship with Christ in His Cross and Resurrection is the profoundest theodicy of all.

Notes

1 Marrou, *St. Augustine and his influence through the ages* (New York: Harper & Bros., 1957), p. 52. "It is because of the anti-Pelagian polemic that he has come down to posterity mainly, or primarily, as the theologian of original sin, predestination and grace, and as the moral teacher on concupiscence and the wretchedness of man when left to his own resources."

2 *Ibid.*, p. 56.

3 Ed. J. Besse, *Dictionnaire de Théologie Catholique,* Paris: Letouzet et Ane Editeurs, 1903), vol. I, a lengthy article by Eugène Portalie on Augustine. The citation is my translation from pp. 2343-2344.

4 One recalls the statement from Augustine that embarrassed Calvin: *Ego vero Evangelio non crederem nisi me Catholicae commoverit avctoritas. (Contra epist. manich., c. 5, n. 6).*

5 *Enchiridion*, 12.

6 *Ibid.*, 11.

7 *Confessions*, VIII, (12) (18).

8 *Enchiridion*, 8 1.

9 *Ibid.*, 3.

10 *St. Augustine and his influence through the ages*, p. 75.

11 *Evil and the God of Love* (New York: Harper & Row, 1966), p. 62.

12 *Learning to live with evil* (Grand Rapids, Michigan: Eerdmans Publishing Co., 1982), pp. 58-9.

13 Hick, *op. cit.*, p. 93.

14 *Enchiridion*, 27.

15 *Evil and the God of Love*, p. 95.

16 See the extensive study by N. P. Williams, *The Ideas of the Fall and of Original Sin* (London: Longmans, Green, 1928).

17 *St. Augustine of Hippo: Life and Controversies* (Philadelphia: Westminster Press, 1963), pp. 373-4. I have derived much benefit from this account marked by subtlety and clarity.

18 *Op. cit.*, p. 374.

19 *De diversis Quaest. ad Simplicianum*, i, q. 2, 20.

20 *De Civ. Dei.*, XIV, xvi.

21 *De Pecc. Orig.*, XXXVII, 42 and XXXIX, 44.

22 Letter 184A, i, 2.

23 *Enchiridion*, 35.

24 *Enchiridion*, 35.

25 *Augustine of Hippo: A Biography* (Berkeley: University of California Press, 1966), p. 403.

26 *De Civ. Dei*, XXI, xii.

27 *De Corrept. et. Grat.*, X, 28.

28 *Ad Simplic.*, i, q. 2, 22.

29 *Serm*, 26, xii. See Eugene Te Selle's claim that Augustine had two theories of predestination, especially that an earlier one indicated that God foresaw the response of faith in some (but not works) and so elected them. Cf. *Augustine the Theologian* (New York: Herder and Herder, 1970), p. 329f.

30 *De Spriritu et littera*, XXV, 45.

31 *Enchiridion*, 47.

32 *Enchiridion*, 34.

33 *Enchiridion*, 32.

34 *Confessions*, X, 29 (40).

35 *Enchiridion*, 98.

36 *De corruptione et gratia*, xiv, 45.

37 *De spiritu et littera*, xxxi, 34.

38 *Augustine of Hippo: A Biography* (Berkeley: University of California Press, 1966), p. 407.

39 I Timothy 2:4.

40 *Contra Julianum*, IV, viii, 44.

41 *Recherches de chronologie augustinienne* (Paris: Etudes Augustiniennes, 1965), p. 180.

42 Epistle 137, 3.

43 Ed. H. Cunliffe-Jones, *A History of Christian Doctrine* (Philadelphia: Fortress Press, 1980), pp. 162-3. The evidence for this judgment comes from *de moribus Manich.* 18:65; *Contra Faust*, 22-30; and *de bono conjug.* 6.

44 *St Augustine of Hippo: Life and Controversies* (Philadelphia: Westminster Press, 1963), p. 390.

45 *Op. cit.*, p. 392. One is reminded of Marrou's reference to "the Terrible Doctor of Predestination for whom, one might say, the shrieks of the damned are only an expressive discord in the chorus of praise given forth by the joys of the elect." (*St. Augustine and his influence through the Ages*, New York: Harper & Bros., 1957), p. 54.

46 Luke 23:34.

47 *Der Augustinismus: eine dogmengeschichtliche studie* (Munchen: J. J. Lentner, 1890), *passim*.

48 *Op. cit.*, 60.

49 *Enchiridion*, 105.

50 *Gratia Christi: Essai d'histoire du Dogme et de théologie dogmatique* (Paris: Beauchesne et ses fils, 1948), p. 140. See *De dono perseverentia*, 16.

51 *Cur ergo, inquit, non omnibus? Et hic respondeo: quoniam Deus judex est. Ibid.*

52 *De Genesis and Litteram*, Ch. 1, para. 3.

53 *Evil and the God of Love* (New York: Harper & Row, 1966), p. 180.

54 *Sighing for Eden* (Nashville Abingdon Press, 1985), pp. 46-47.

55 *Enchiridion*, 27.

56 I have availed myself substantially of the brilliant summary of Professor Hick in this paragraph. *Op. cit.*, pp. 199-200.

Chapter 3

St. Thomas Aquinas's Doctrine of Providence

St. Thomas Aquinas, like St. Augustine, was a philosophical theologian, but while Augustine drew upon the philosophy of Plato and the neo-Platonists, Aquinas made use of the philosophy of Aristotle and of some Neo-Aristotelians. He used the Arab philosopher Avicenna, and the Jewish philosopher Maimonides, while also fighting the philosophical interpretation of Aristotle offered by another Arab philosopher, Averroes.[1] Like Augustine in another respect, he modified and adapted what he borrowed to fit the Christian revelation.

Aquinas was also greatly indebted to Augustine and quoted him with greater frequency than any other of the Fathers of the Church. But in approach and in formulating and inventing new genres (the *Confessions* and the philosophy of history—*The City of God*), as well as in his rhetorical brilliance, St. Augustine seems more original than St. Thomas. Still, if it comes to sustained consistency, encyclopedic treatment and cool rationality, with analytic depth and logical rigor, Aquinas remains unequalled.

1. His Growing Posthumous Fame

While involved in many controversies like Augustine, St. Thomas's fame grew astonishingly after his death, leading to his early canonization on July 18, 1323, almost fifty years later. It peaked in the Encyclical of Leo XII of 1879, *Aeterni Patris*, which included the praise: "human reason soared to the loftiest heights on the wings of Thomas and can scarcely rise any higher, while faith can expect no further more reliable assistance than such as it has already received from Thomas." There was even further Papal approval for Aquinas in Pius X's Encyclical, *Ducem* of 1923, recommending St. Thomas as the foremost theological teacher of the Catholic Church.[2]

Meanwhile, Neo-Thomism had developed, particularly in France under the aegis of Jacques Maritain, Etienne Gilson and M. D. Chenu, O.P. Maritain insisted that the study of Aquinas was no mere medieval and romantic anachronism, and his admiration reached this paean of praise: "We know that the wisdom of St. Thomas is running on the highways of the world before the footsteps of God . . . Our whole task is to prepare a way of approach to it. For this reason I have said and I repeat: *Vae mihi, si non thomistizavero.*"[3] (Woe is me if I do not thomisticize.)

The importance of the teaching of St. Thomas Aquinas and its dominant role in the Catholic Church is attested by the honorific titles which he received. He has been called the *Angelic Doctor,* an indication both of his holy life and towering intelligence, resembling that of the angels on whose hierarchy and quality he had written extensively. Also he has been named the *Doctor of the Eucharist* because it is believed that he was invited to compose for the feast of *Corpus Domini* (the Body of the Lord) the prayers and hymns of the Eucharist, and another Pope six centuries later gave him the title.[4] But his greatest name indicating his universal significance for the Latin Church is that of *Common Doctor (Doctor Communis).*[5]

Yet in his own time he was fiercely criticized as well as applauded. This is the man whose reputation was castigated by the Bishop of Paris, because of Thomas's Aristotelianism, so that he was officially condemned in 1377. This included many of the officially Thomist theses. Yet what other philosopher has ever been celebrated by the most famous poet of the Middle Ages? M. C. D'Arcy writes that after Thomas's canonization his fame became universal: "the proof is that the greatest poet of the Middle Ages enshrined that philosophy in verse. Never has any other philosopher had such good fortune or been made so sure of immortality. Dante did not by any means like all the heroes of the age, but there is no doubt of his admiration for St. Thomas"[6] whom he makes the spokesman of the theologians—those burning lights that are "like the stars in the neighbourhood of the steadfast poles."

2. The Variety of His Writings

Two other clues to his importance are the length and variety of his writings (he died at fifty and had written forty books) and the vast number of translations, commentaries and biographies of Aquinas, termed "the Aquinas industry." The genres of his works include two vast syntheses of *Summae*: the *Summa contra Gentiles* and the *Summa Theologiae*: commentaries on the Bible,[7] Dionysius, Boethius and Aristotle, a study of Peter Lombard and an exposition correlating the four Gospels and a number of opuscules of a philosophical, theological or devotional nature.[8]

Then there are treatments of two types of *Disputed Questions*. The first kind is works prepared for ordinary disputations between himself as Master and the university scholars who sat under his teaching. These number 63 distributed under 7 titles: *De Veritate* (Concerning the Truth); *De Potentia Dei* (Concerning God's Power); *De malo* (Concerning Evil); *De spiritualibus creaturis* (Concerning spiritual creatures); *De anima* (Concerning the soul); *De virtutibus* (Concerning the virtues); and the *De unione Verbi incarnati* (Concerning the union of the incarnate Word).

The second group of *Disputed Questions* are known as the *Quodlibeta Series*, in which those attending included other regent masters of the university as well as the pupils. There were no holds barred. The series VII to XI were free-for-all questions and the answers were given by Thomas as regent master in Paris for the first time from 1256-59; while the second set of *Quodlibeta* Questions with Aquinas's answers were given when he taught there a second time, from 1269-72. The academic session taking the form of a disputation, and which was known as the *quaestio de quolibet*, is characterized by M.-D. Chenu as "a session in which the multiplicity and heterogeneity of the questions raised and the unforeseeable form the participation of those present took, gave these disputations a very original and extraordinary animated air."[9]

The greatest significance of St. Thomas as a philosophical theologian is, however, found in his elaboration of the capacity of reason to establish a natural theology. No one has gone as far as he in this direction without calling upon the mysteries of the supernatural Christian revelation–such as the Trinity, the

Incarnation, the Passion, the Resurrection and the Ascension of Christ. Moreover, he saw natural theology as a bridge leading from reason to faith in the Divine special revelation, and insisted that there can be no conflict in the knowledge of God derived from the two different sources of reason and revelation. He summed it up thus: "Between Reason which comes from God, and a Revelation which comes from God, accord must be of necessity."[10] In his belief in a natural knowledge of God attainable by reason, he could not be farther apart from the theological approach of Karl Barth or of that of any other Protestant theologian. But, oddly enough, Barth resembles him in two ways: in an absorbing interest in angels, their hierarchical orders, and their functions as Divine messengers to humans, as recorded in the Bible, and in leaving his lengthy *magnum opus* incomplete.

3. St. Thomas's Character

Saint Thomas is like a many-faceted and shining diamond of the purest quality. As a saint, perhaps Gilson's is the best description of him in the words: "Never perhaps has a more exacting intellect responded to the call of so religious a heart."[11] It is highly significant that his parents would have greatly preferred him to be a Benedictine because a relative of theirs was the Abbot of the most prestigious abbey of Monte Cassino, founded by St. Benedict himself, and thus they would gain influence in the struggle between Papacy and Empire which was acute in their time and in their neighborhood. But Thomas refused even the possible compromise of continuing to wear the habit of a Dominican while holding a Benedictine abbacy. For him it was precisely the privilege of imitating Christ and the disciples as a mendicant friar that was the center of the appeal of St. Dominic to him in the earliest years of the Order of Preachers. Yet family pressure was mounting: he was captured by his own brothers while on his way to an important council in the company of the master-general of the order. He was secluded in one of the family castles, tempted by a seductive girl pushed into his room, and for a whole year his mother tried to persuade him to leave the Dominicans. Later he was even offered the Archbishopric of Naples. But nothing could shake his indomitable determination to remain a mendicant preaching friar.[12] Such was the holiness of St. Thomas.

Despite his intellectual distinction, he was a man of the deepest humility. This is made plain by two stories.

While at a meal with another great Saint, Louis IX, King of France, he became so absorbed in a discussion that he forgot all decorum and banged his massive hand on the table and shouted: "Now I have an argument with which to defeat the Manichean heretics!" It is pleasant to report that Saint Louis was not offended but immediately called for his secretary so that St. Thomas could dictate the argument in detail before it would be lost for ever.[13]

The second story illustrating his humility was recorded in the proceedings for his canonization. Incidentally, it illustrates the fierce differences between the Franciscans and the Dominicans in Paris in relation to the teaching of Aristotle. The master regent of the Friars Minor, John Peckham, (later to be Archbishop of Canterbury), stood up to attack the master regent of the Dominicans, Thomas Aquinas, in the presence of all the bachelors and masters. He sharply criticized the account Thomas had given of the Aristotelian theory of the unity of forms. Then, the report states "that however much the said Brother John, in his pompous and inflated terms [*verbis ampullosis et tumidis*], showed himself aggravating to the same Brother Thomas, not once did the latter himself cease to use the language of humility, but was always pleasant and humane in his answers."[14]

4. A Biographical Sketch

Before any consideration of the developed and systematic thought of Thomas Aquinas, we must provide the briefest of biographies as well as a very summary account of the temporal and geographical context in which he lived. It will then be more meaningful to describe and assess his doctrine of Providence, which is a wide-ranging one.

The exact year of his birth we do not know, but William of Tocco, his earliest reliable biographer, affirms that Thomas "was in the 49th year of his life"[15] when he died, thus meaning that he had passed his forty-eighth birthday, but not yet his forty-ninth. He was born in the castle of Roccasecca near to Monte Cassino to parents of the smaller nobility, being the seventh son. In 1239 a new abbot, no relation to Thomas, sent the oblates to the Benedictine house in Naples so that they might complete their studies at the imperial University of Naples founded only 25 years before by Frederick II as a rival to Bologna. It was here that Aquinas was first introduced to Aristotelianism by an admirable teacher, Peter of Ireland, who, at the emperor's court had been encouraged to study the newly-arriving Greek and Arabic translations and commentaries on the physics and metaphysics of Aristotle.[16] Hitherto Aristotle had been known in the West for his logic and his ethics, but not for these other works, which came as a shock to the Neo-Platonic and conservative Augustinian Franciscans.[17] The most able religious and philosophic mind of this group was St. Bonaventure.

While at the University of Naples, Aquinas became attracted to the Dominicans with their concept of evangelical poverty, combined with study and service to the Church without ecclesiastical preferments.[18] In the summer of 1245 he returned to the Friars at Naples after an imbroglio with his family.

Between 1245 and 1252 he undertook further studies at Paris and in Cologne, where he had the great advantage of being taught for four years by Albert (later honoured as "Saint Albert the Great") who had made five paraphrases of Aristotle's works and the encyclopedic *Summa de creaturis*. Albert soon saw the potentiality of Thomas as a thinker. This quiet young man, it is said, prepared a very faithful record of Albert's lectures. It may be true that his student colleagues in Cologne dubbed him a "dumb ox" (*bovem mutum*), but legend tells us that hearing of this nickname, St. Albert retorted: "Yes, but his roaring will be heard throughout Europe."[19]

In 1252 Aquinas was back in Paris and by 1256 had gained his master's degree in theology, which required a papal dispensation for he was under age. For the next three years he taught theology as a regent master of the university. Wider recognition brought further responsibilities, and so in June of 1259 he was invited to Valenciennes to assist in the proposal and organization of a curriculum in the liberal arts to be approved by the Order at their chapter. For the rest of that year he stayed in Paris, and began writing his famous *Summa contra Gentiles*, which, because of the other calls on his time, would not be completed until the fall of 1264.

At the end of 1259 he left Paris for Naples. He remained there until the fall of 1261 working on the missionary *Summa*. He was then called as a *lector* (reader) of his Order to Orvieto, where he remained for the next four years. This city was the headquarters of Pope Urban the Fourth, to whom he became an important advisor. During these years he also managed to complete the five Books of the *Summa contra Gentiles* and very probably also the Form of worship for the newly-founded celebration of the Feast of Corpus Christi, including the choice of lections, the prayers, and the outstanding hymns, especially the *Adoro te devote*[20]. Also at Papal request he prepared the *Catena Aurea*, (or Golden Chain)[21] and the *Contra errores Graecorum*.[22]

In 1266 Thomas was assigned to open a study center (*studium generale*) for Dominicans in Rome. The very next year he began what was to prove his masterpiece, The *Summa Theologiae*, which, although unfinished, contained 38 treatises, 3,000 articles, and ten thousand objections which he answered.[23] Understandably, to proceed thus far in his major work took him from 1266 to 1273.

In recognition of his importance he was sent back to the University of Paris to be, for the second time, regent master in theology, when there was a bitter fight between the pro-Aristotle faction in the Faculty of Arts who accepted the rationalistic interpretations of the Arab Averroes, and the conservative Friars Minor as Augustinians. These anti-Aristotelians were backed by St. Bonaventure, and their spokesman, we may recall, was John Peckham. Aquinas' regency lasted from January 1269 to 1272, and at the end of his second year the Bishop of Paris made a public condemnation of Averroism[24] which included 12 tenets of Aquinas's interpretation of Aristotle. The condemnation was renewed in Paris in 1377 as well as at Oxford. So, although Thomas was dead, he was doubly discredited for his moderate Aristotelianism, because it was wrongly linked with the skeptical rationalism of the interpretations of Aristotle offered by Siger of Brabant[25] and Boethius of Dacia.[26]

The fundamental difficulty in trying to "Christianize" Aristotle was twofold: by asserting the eternity of the world Aristotle's thought conflicted with Jewish and Christian Biblical teaching of the creation by God in time with its recognition of humanity made in the image of God and dependent on Him, and the interpretation by Averroes of Aristotle, credited him with asserting that the intellect which abstracted information from sensory experience (the so-called *active intellect*) and the intellect as the storehouse of ideas (the so-called *passive intellect*) was an entity shared by the human race as a whole instead of being an individual possession, which had the consequence of undermining any conviction of personal immortality.[27] In addition, the eternal world of Aristotle was controlled by determinism which was without a provident God who knew anything of human contingencies. This unmoved Mover would be deaf to human prayers, and human beings themselves were beings bound up with matter, and like matter, bound to corruption. No wonder that this empiricism first aroused fear, which led later to the appreciation of Aristotle's marvelous comprehensiveness in the understanding of physics, biology, politics, metaphysics, and logic, as well as ethics. Thomas Aquinas, like Albert the Great, saw that *the* Philosopher could not be ignored or dismissed, but had to be "purged" (Maritain's term), or, perhaps better, "tamed" for a new life in theological circles, a very daring decision.

5. The Death of Aquinas

After his second troubled regency in Paris, Aquinas left for Florence and in September 1272 became, presumably with great relief, regent in theology at the University of Naples. However, as a result of the previous mental strain and exhaustion from his indefatigable labors in writing he had what may be regarded variously as a breakdown, a stroke, or a mystical experience, or even a combination of all three, which forced him to discontinue his writing of the great *Summa Theologiae* on December 6, 1273. He still set out for the Second Council of Lyons, convened by the new Pope Gregory X to reconcile the Greeks with the Latin Church, early in 1274. While on the way Aquinas seems to have hit his head on an obstructing bough of a tree at Borgonuevo, and then stayed for a few days at the castle of his niece in Maenza, where he became steadily worse. He was heard to say, "If the Lord is coming for me, I had better be found in a religious house than in a castle." He then asked to be taken to the nearby Cistercian monastery of Fossanova at the end of February. Brought up by Benedictines, he received his viaticum at Benedictine hands and on the 7th of March 1274, in the morning, he died. On March 9th, he was buried in front of the high altar of the chapel.

The most surprising of the events in the last year of his life was his discontinuance of the *Summa Theologiae*. On Wednesday morning, the Feast of St. Nicholas, December 6th, Thomas got up early as usual to celebrate the Mass of the feast in the chapel of St. Nicholas, during which he was suddenly struck by something that profoundly changed him (*mira mutatione*). When his friend Reginald realized that Thomas had radically altered his routine of over fifteen years, he inquired, "Father, why have you laid aside such a great work which you began for the praise of God and the world's enlightenment?" Thomas simply answered, "Reginald, I cannot." Reginald repeated his question, and in return received the following reply: "Reginald, I cannot, because all that I have written seems like straw to me." The conclusion of Father James Weisheipl, his best modern biographer, is that there was a combination of a breakdown (both mental and physical) and a mystical experience. He adds that "In divine providence such a disturbance of mind and body is sometimes accompanied by a mystical experience . . . and, in Thomas's case, the two aspects could have been simultaneous: everything he had done and worked for seemed 'worthless', 'trivial', and 'like straw.'"[28]

It is not surprising that the start of an Oxford manuscript of the *Summa Theologiae* records the following words: "Here Thomas dies. O Death, how thou art accursed!"[29] So remarkable a thinker who had "purged" Aristotle for use in Christian apologetics, devout poet, admirable member of the Order of Preaching Friars, utterly disinterested in ecclesiastical preferment, yet adviser to Popes and monarchs, exciting and daring lecturer in the universities of Paris and Naples, and brilliant dialectician, and superb analyst: it was the loss of a theological giant. But, and this must be stated before we examine his thought on the doctrine of Divine Providence, he was the right man at the right time in the right places.

This has been excellently and succinctly expressed by M.-D. Chenu in the following paragraph, which only needs to add that Thomas's enthusiasm for Aristotle was developed prior to his study with Albert the Great by his earlier instruction in Naples by Peter of Ireland:

> "It is not unimportant that, in the days of Saint Louis and Frederick II, Saint Thomas should arrive on Paris at a time:
>
> when, in a new society just entered upon a communal era, it was in the corporate university body that intellectual eagerness and curiosity were concentrated and were to introduce Aristotle and ancient reason to Christian thought;
>
> when the cathedral of Notre Dame of Paris was being completed and the *Romance of the Rose* written;
>
> when, after the battle of Bouvines wherein the Holy Roman Empire and its feudal hierarchy were jointly defeated (1214), Europe was entering on a new era in which it would cease to be a theocratic entity;
>
> when the Moslems were hemming in the Western world by their military successes and seducing it by their science and philosophy;
>
> when, finally, merchants and missionaries were pushing their way into Cathay and discovering the world's dimensions and the variety of its civilizations.
>
> Neither is it unimportant that Saint Thomas should join the Friar Preachers in the Christian World of Innocent III and that he should find in the midst of this new religious family, at the most opportune time, an Albert the Great to be his master."[30]

6. Aquinas's Thought Introduced

The concept of Providence required the context of Aquinas's life and times. It also needs a general introduction to his thought. This will involve five brief considerations:

(i) of the two approaches to the knowledge of God by reason (the negative way and the way of analogy);

(ii) the Five Ways or Arguments for the existence of God;

(iii) the complementary roles of reason (in philosophy) and faith (in theology utilizing the Divine mysteries conveyed in the Bible and the Church's Creeds); both important, but both inferior to the vision of God directly attained in the state of Beatitude in eternity in God's immediate Presence;

(iv) Absolute Being and the grades of being as they descend from God, through angels to human beings, thence to animals, plants, and inanimate nature in which St. Thomas borrows from the Neo-Platonist, the Pseudo-Dionysius; and, finally,

(v) the important structures of the *Summa Contra Gentiles* and the *Summa Theologiae* which mirror a descent of God to humanity and a corresponding return of humanity to God effected through the Incarnation, and it is these *Summae* which will provide almost the whole of St. Thomas's teaching on the ever-vigilant Providence of God.

(i) Contrary to the Augustinian Neo-Platonists who believed that by illuminism they had a direct knowledge of God, Aquinas, following Aristotle's empiricism (requiring intellection through sensate experience), insisted that the approach to God must be largely negative in character. He explained his negative method as follows: "The existence of a thing having been ascertained, the way in which it exists remains to be examined, if we would know its nature. Because we cannot know what God is but rather what God is not, our method has to be mainly negative . . . What kind of being God is not can be known by eliminating characteristics which cannot apply to Him, like composition, change and so forth."[31] Since we cannot attain to a knowledge of the Divine essence, for that evades our human grasp because of its immensity, we can only attempt to grasp what it is *not*.

Both *Summae* and the *Compedium Theologiae* and their deductions are drawn from the first argument of Thomas, which he drew from Aristotle, of God as the First Mover, Himself Unmoved, consequently, immobile, thus having neither beginning nor end and so eternal, since the notion of time is eliminated from the Divine essence. Since God is eternal, therefore

He cannot *not* be, which excludes potentiality in Him. Consequently He is pure act (*actus purus*). Also He must be immaterial (since matter is in potency and change), and simple, that is, lacking all composition.[32] Since He is non-composite, He cannot contain anything forcibly imposed on Him, or against His nature.[33] Since He is not a body,[34] (every body contains parts), the idolatrous pagans as well as the Manichaean dualists and the Greek philosophers are thereby refuted who erroneously substituted celestial bodies or the elements for God. A further consequence of the Divine simplicity is that God is His own essence;[35] the nature of the existence of all other beings in the cosmos is, therefore, derived and dependent upon God. Since the Divine substance is Being itself, it possesses nothing which is derived outside itself, and cannot, therefore, contain any accident.[36] Nor could it be possible to define God by any substantial difference or to subsume God as a species under any genus whatever, hence God is ultimately undefinable, because all definitions are attained by the use of genus and differences. The only adequate proofs of God's existence must, therefore, be *a posteriori*, that is, from God's effects. Thus *a priori* proofs from His essence are rightly rejected by Aquinas.[37]

Since, in Gilson's phrase, the affirmations just made are only "disguised negations"[38] it would be desirable to examine what can be said about God in the analogical manner, itself dependent upon the analogy or proportion between the Creator and the creatures, for there are resemblances in all things on which God confers their perfections, and yet also there are unlikenesses to God as well. So when positive statements are made concerning God, the words which we use to describe God and the creatures of God are not used in the same sense; that is univocal predication is not possible, nor is equivocal, but only analogical or proportional predication. St. Thomas explains: "in the terms which we predicate of God, there are two things to consider, namely, the actual perfections signified, like goodness, life, and so forth, and the mode of significance. As regards the former, these belong properly to God, indeed more properly than to creatures, and the terms are predicated primarily of God, but as regards the mode of signification, they are not properly predicated of God. For they have a mode of predication that belongs to creatures."[39] Thus, wisdom and goodness and being and love are perfect and unitary in God, but in human beings they are considerably weaker. For this reason Copleston says there is in Aquinas an epistemological "agnosticism" in the human knowledge of God,[40] which is clearly acknowledged by Aquinas in the statement: "The first cause surpasses human understanding and speech. He knows God best who acknowledges that whatever he thinks and says falls short of what God really is."[41]

Nevertheless, starting from the absolute perfection of God, demands that we recognize that He must include goodness in His perfectness.[42] Also among the perfections of creatures, which are also from God, because He combines all perfections, we must also predicate intelligence and will,[43] the former proving His supreme Wisdom as Omniscient and the latter His Omnipotence. Since it is accompanied with Goodness it is omniscient, omnipotent, beneficent Providence. Moreover, in this insistence upon God's omniscience, reflected although in an inferior fashion in human beings, Aquinas was insisting on two important anti-Averroistic conclusions. These were that God in knowing Himself also knew all things, even particulars,[44] and God even knows future contingencies, not successively as they are realized in time, but simultaneously, since He is above them. In this way He is providential.[45]

(ii) We now move from epistemology to consider Aquinas's Five Proofs of the existence of God which he modestly calls "Ways" rather than demonstrative proofs. One might well ask why Thomas Aquinas finds it necessary to provide such proofs. Copleston suggests two reasons for doing so: first, this is natural in a preamble to faith in the type of systematic theology that the *Summa Theologiae* represents; secondly, God's existence is obviously not self-evident to the agnostic and atheists of the world.[46] Indeed, Aquinas admits this is the case: "No one can think the opposite of that which is self-evident . . . But the opposite of the proposition 'God exists' can be thought, therefore the proposition 'God exists' can be thought . . . therefore the proposition that God exists is not self-evident."[47]

Thomas rejects the Anselmic *a priori* proof that to assert that God "Who is that than which nothing greater can be conceived" would be a self-contradiction. He has five arguments in the *Summa Theologiae* all dependent on different causes whose effects are known in experience, and thus each shows a different aspect of Divine causality. The first proof displays God as the efficient cause of cosmic movement, while the second manifests God as the cause of the existence of things, and is dependent upon a hierarchical view of beings in which the lower are dependent upon the higher. The third proof distinguishes between the possible and the necessary, and depends on two premises: first, the possible, which can be or *not* be, is contrasted with the necessary which must be, and the second is that the possible derives its existence not from itself but from a higher efficient cause which gives existence to the possible. All three deny the possibility of an infinite regress to arrive at God. The fourth proof is founded on the Degree of Being, since we experience things comparatively as having more or less than the supreme degree of being (as, for example, some things are true, good, noble, and so on), and consequently something exists which combines all these perfections, and this is what we call God. Here the Platonic and Augustinian idea of participation in ultimate Being is utilized. The fifth proof comes from the government of things, or, in other words, assumes Providence, and, for our purposes, warrants fuller treatment.

The concept of God as the universe's Ruler was, of course, common to the three monotheistic faiths of Judaism, Christianity, and Islam. St. Thomas in the *Summa Contra Gentiles* refers us to the model for his proof, namely, St. John of Damascus in his *De Fide Orthodoxa* (On the Orthodox Faith).[48] The argument takes the following form: it is the presence of a being ordering them that harmonizes and reconciles opposed and disparate things. The same ordered arrangement is necessary to account for this government, with its direction of all together and each thing separately towards a definite end. We observe in the world that things with different natures are, in fact, harmonized, not just occasionally or rarely, but if not always, for most of the time. Therefore, there must exist a being by whose providence the world is governed, and this Being we call God.[49] This argument is based on God as the final cause, as the others were on God as first cause. In the *Summa Theologiae* it is thus arranged in Thomas's own words: "The fifth way is taken from the government of the world. We see that things which lack knowledge, such as natural bodies, act for an end, and this is evident from their acting always or nearly always, in the same way, so as to obtain the best result. Hence it is plain that they achieve their end, not fortuitously, but designedly. Now whatever lacks knowledge cannot move towards an end, unless it be directed by some being endowed with knowledge and intelligence; as the arrow is directed by the archer. Therefore, some intelligent being exists by whom all natural things are directed to their end; and this being we call God."[50] The significant difference between the two presentations of the argument is that the second presumes an intelligence directing the order of the universe. This Gilson rightly interprets: "the thought inherent in things is explained, as are the things themselves by the imitation from afar of the thought of the Divine providence that rules them."[51]

All five proofs make use of the causal inference, for the concept of cause is for Aquinas a first principle. Since, as we shall see, Thomas affirms a hierarchy of beings, a regression to infinity in a whole series of causes permits reason to affirm the existence of God. And if the reason for one existence can be made in empirical terms, then the existence of God can be proved. Furthermore, God is the first cause, not merely because He initiates everything and is its final end, but because essence and existence are one in Him. Hence He would only be caused if His essence were distinct from His existence. Therefore He must be the first cause.[52] So God's essence is the act of being, and hence, Who is, is the proper name of God, as Exodus 3:14 attests. It is interesting that St. Augustine saw God as never changing, but Thomas sees God as He who is the pure act of being.[53]

If we are to interpret St. Thomas correctly, we must realize that when he speaks of an infinite regress, he does not mean this in any way to imply that we are to imagine a "linear or horizontal series, but a vertical hierarchy, in which a lower member depends here and now on the present causal activity of the member above it . . . and the word 'first' does not mean first in temporal order, but supreme or first in the ontological order."[54]

Copleston points out that even if we allow that there is a first or supreme unmoved Mover (as Aristotle did), a first efficient cause, and an absolutely necessary Being, it does not necessarily follow that such a being is appropriately called 'God'. There are, however, two answers to this criticism. The first is to recall that the fifth argument posits an intelligent transmundane being, and that in the fourth argument there is also posited a perfect being possessing the perfection of intelligence. Furthermore, if the conclusion of the five ways is that there is a supreme intelligent Being, then this Being must transcend the level of empirical causes effected by it, and is unmoved, uncaused and independent. Also, it is true to say that such a being, transcendent, supreme and uncaused cause is the One that all who acknowledge such a Being "call this being God," as Thomas affirms. St. Thomas vivifies the conception of God by his discussion of the Divine Attributes in the negative and analogical ways.[55] Here we have in Father Copleston a distinguished Jesuit philosopher and historian making out a good case for the defense of St. Thomas. If an effective philosophical prosecutor is required he can be found in Dr. Anthony Kenny, formerly Master of Balliol College, Oxford, who has produced a devastating critique of each of the five proofs.[56]

(iii) By a natural transition, we move from an attempted rational series of demonstrative proofs of the existence of God to discover the roles that St. Thomas gives to reason and faith, and to the two distinct "sciences" which he gives the name of theology, *scientia divina* (Divine knowledge) and *scientia dei* (knowledge of God). The former is a series of propositions which results from philosophical reflection on the part of human beings using the natural powers of reason. This is also known as "natural theology" although this term was not used for the *Scientia divina* by St. Thomas,[57] but is a commonplace of present day theological discussion. *Scientia dei* is built upon a series of propositions which are available from revelation and are derived from Scripture.[58] They include such mysteries as The Trinity, Creation, the Incarnation and the Eucharist. Thus Thomas distinguishes between a philosophical theology which is metaphysics and a theology of Holy Scripture, which is theology proper.[59]

The points of difference between the two correlated disciplines or sciences will be summarized by making a series of contrasts, but with the overriding recognition that for St. Thomas divine science and the science of God are complementary and cannot contradict each other. They are both inferior to the ultimate knowledge and love of God in the final vision of God attainable in eternity.

The divine science is philosophy (and chiefly metaphysics). It becomes knowable by the interior light of the *intellectus agens* (active intellect) and is presented to the intellect by the senses. This natural activity apprehends in sensible things the *ratio entis* (the essence or reason for existence) in which the first principles are based and the quiddities of observable substances by the mode of abstraction. The true or proper subject of metaphysics is being as such, and God is known as the necessary cause of this subject. In addition, we learn of Him by the way of negation what He is by what He is not.[60] Also, in the strictest sense, neither in philosophy nor in theology, do we reach a knowledge of what God is (*quid est*) but only a cognition *that* He is (*an est*).

In contrast, theology or the science of God, is that which becomes believable through the operation of the light of faith. It is presented to the intellect by Holy Scripture and the articles of faith, and both are the expression of an historic revelation. The light of faith enables the intellect to apprehend the God who reveals Himself, not in His essence, "but in His salvation value, by means of a supernatural instinct" which "gives . . . by way of connaturality, a sympathy, an inner discernment of the divine truth, and this infallibly moves him [man] to assent."[61] God's attraction lies behind the human desire for knowledge, whether theological or philosophical.[62] As a discipline the science of God is even more certain than philosophy, partly because philosophers make mistakes and differ from one another,[63] and the necessary training and application restrict the reflection to a very small minority (*paucis hominibus*) of the population;[64] but mainly it is because the light of divine revelation by which we participate in the science of God cannot deceive.[65] Therefore, St. Thomas maintains the necessity of revelation for all questions of ultimate concern: "Hence it was necessary for the salvation of man that certain truths which exceed human reason should be made known to him by divine revelation. For the truth about God, as reason can know it, would only be known by a few, and that after a long time, and with the admixture of many errors; whereas man's whole salvation, which is in God, depends upon the knowledge of this truth."[66]

One can hardly fail to be impressed by the way the emphasis on knowledge and reason runs through the system of Aquinas, and this is admirably expressed in the penultimate sentence of Per Erik Persson's analysis of the relation of reason and revelation: "The cognitive aspect in taking *fides* [faith] as the starting-point is emphasized by the fact that Thomas regards theology as a *scientia,* and in this sense therefore a continuous line extends from natural knowledge, through the imperfect anticipation of the beatific vision in theology, to the *beatitudo* [beatitude, or blessedness] which is man's final end, and which at one time represents the fullness of knowledge, man's own highest perfection, and the absolute climax of revelation." [67]

(iv) The last quotation inevitably suggests our next subject: namely, the importance of the different grades or levels of being in the thought of Aquinas. There is, of course, a residual neo-Platonism in the conception of the hierarchy of beings, and St. Thomas did, in fact, write commentaries on works of the Pseudo-Dionysius who was erroneously thought in the Middle Ages to be a disciple of St. Paul, which gave him theological stature. Thomas cites him frequently, indeed, more than 1700 times![68] And it is probable that an extant manuscript in typically almost illegible handwriting contains Thomas's lecture transcript of the lectures that Albert the Great gave on Dionysius in Paris in 1247 and afterwards in Cologne.[69] At first it seemed, because of the Neo-Platonist's emphasis on the sensible, Aquinas thought he was an Aristotelian, but later he interpreted the metaphysics of good (Dionysius) as concurring with the metaphysics of being (Aristotle). His final conviction, as Etienne Gilson has shown, is found in the *De Causis,* where he declares: "According to the Platonists, the prime cause is in fact above being inasmuch as the essence of goodness and of oneness, which the prime cause is, surpasses separate being itself, as was stated above; according to truth, however, the prime cause is above being inasmuch as it is infinite being itself."[70] The important commentaries on Dionysius the Areopagite prepared by Aquinas are *De Divinis Nominibus* (On the Divine Names) and the *Liber de Causis* (Book of Causes).

The result was that the hierarchy of beings, begins with God as the Supreme Being, at the top, with all the perfections, and in descending order and imitating Him in successively lower modes are the angels, who are pure intelligences. At a level immediately below them are human beings, who are embodied intelligences and use their intellect in abstraction from sensation, and also have wills capable of free choice and have appetites. Below them are animals which have some knowledge but are chiefly sensate beings, and below them are plants with inferior sensation, and rocks that are inanimate. All these levels of being have their end in God, as also their origin, and they are created in their way to be attracted by and assimilated to God. The only explanation the human mind can offer of the exodus of these perfections from God to creatures, says Thomas, is that the good tends naturally to diffuse itself beyond itself and therefore to communicate itself to other beings to the degree that they are capable of receiving it.[71] And what is true of any good, as we know it, is in an eminent degree true of the Supreme Good, God.

Angels, or pure spirits, are the highest order of creatures and they are such because they are incorporeal, unlike human beings with bodies since as material humans are determined for a particular and therefore non-universal mode of being. But the Divine Providence has so arranged that they are, in their three hierarchies, inclusive of lower angels who are messengers of God to humanity,[72] and if they did not exist there would be no beings intermediate between God and humans.[73] Man is a union of soul and body, and hence the human intellect requires a body to achieve its proper activation, and so is inferior to the pure intellectuality of the angel.[74] Man also has feelings as well as intellectual acts, so he is a composite of soul and body. The human soul is therefore on the frontier between spirits and bodies,[75] and the powers of both are combined in it.[76]

The powers of the soul are intellectual, sensitive, and vegetative. The active intellect is one of the powers of the human soul,[77] and its function is to render intelligible what is potentially so in sensible reality.[78] The soul also possesses capacities for willing and desiring. The Divine Creation involves two acts: one is the bringing forth of all things from God, and the second is the impulse to return to God, the first Source. God is both the efficient cause, as He is the final end, and for humans, that is beatitude, knowing God who alone can satisfy the will and the intellect as both love and intellectual vision. This is found only in the life to come where the soul receives immortal perfection,[79] and shares in mutual joy.[80] This offers us pilgrims, still on the way, a glimpse of what the providence of God has prepared for those who live by the obedience of faith.

(v) Finally, as preparation for the rich understanding of Providence as outlined by St. Thomas, we must consider, most concisely, the structures of the *Summa Contra Gentiles* and of the *Summa Theologiae*. It has already been hinted at, and it is the surest indication of the Divine vigilance and compassionate care for humanity. It is the Divine Circle or parabola by which the effects of God, as First Cause come *down* to humanity, and the desire of humanity for the goodness, the truth, and the love of God which draw humankind back to God as the final end, assisted by the Incarnation in which God descends in the person of the Word and second Person of the Holy Trinity to human level to demonstrate the way back, prepares the individual for the ascent to Blessedness in the Vision of God and the company of all the saints in eternity.

The *Summa Contra Gentiles* is more than a missionary book, although it is that, but it is a defense of Christian thought confronted by a series of intelligent erring thinkers, such as the famous pagans, as well as the Moslems, the Jews, and the heretics who are all censured after an examination of their views. Its alternative title in many manuscripts indicates its apologetical purpose: *Liber de veritate catholicae fidei contra errores infidelium* (A Book on the Truth of the Catholic Faith against the errors of the unbelievers). The order, according to Thomas, of the first three books, is theological: "But in the teaching of faith, which does not consider creatures except in their relation to God, the consideration of God comes first, and afterwards the consideration of creatures . . . And so, in accordance with this order, after what has been said in Book I about God in Himself, there remains to continue with the things that come from Him."[81]

In the *Summa Theologiae* the purpose is clarified in the prologue: "Because the Doctor of Catholic truth must teach not only the advanced student, but to him also devolves the task of instructing beginners . . . we intend in the present work to impart the matters that pertain to the Christian religion in such a way as may benefit the instruction of beginners."

If we look beyond the logical structure with its divisions and subdivisions, objections to theses and answers to objections, we shall find that the inner architecture or structure, like that of the *Contra Gentiles* is again a reflection of the Divine Circle or Parabola. The stress is in emphasizing emanation from God and return to God, and looks oddly neo-Platonic. Yet, as M.-D. Chenu insists, this is precisely what its three Parts envisage: "*Ia Pars*–emanation from God–the principle; *IIa Pars*–return to God–the end; and because, *de facto*, by God's free and utterly gratuitous design (sacred history reveals this to us) this return is effected through Christ–the man-God, a *IIIa Pars* will study the "Christian conditions of the return."[82] And in Thomas's own words here is the plan: "Because the chief aim of sacred doctrine is to impart the knowledge of God, not only as He is in Himself, but also as He is the beginning of things and their end, especially of rational creatures . . . in our endeavour to expound this doctrine, we shall treat (1) of God; (2) of the movement of rational creatures to God; (3) of Christ, Who, as man, is our Way to God."[83]

7. The Providence in the *Summa Contra Gentiles*

Finally, after preliminary clues as to the descending levels of being from God to the creatures, and to God as First Cause and Final Causes, with Christ the God-man as Mediator of salvation, we reach Thomas's detailed consideration of Providence in Book III and Chapters 64-100 in the *Summa contra Gentiles*,[84] which we must summarize. Thomas will treat of the three major aspects of Providence: Creation, with the consequence of the dependence of all creatures upon God and man made in His image with intelligence and will; the Divine preservation of all living things (*Sustentatio* or *Preservatio*); and, what chiefly attracts Thomas's wondering gratitude, namely, God's Government of the universe (*Gubernatio*) in its marvelous ordering. Aquinas will, of course, have to deal with evil, which seems to contradict, or at least, hinder and obstruct the Divine order and benevolence, and, in fact, he had earlier acknowledged the existence of evil,[85] arguing that it was unintentional since it is merely a privation of goodness, and consequently, a defect of being and of goodness.[86]

The concentration on Providence begins with the title of Chapter 64: "That God Governs Things by His Providence." Here we reach the mind and heart of Aquinas on this theme. As illustration of the government of God, he takes an army and its general devoted to obtaining victory as its end, and controlling many units and lesser powers for the good of the whole. Since he has previously shown that all things are directed to the divine goodness as their last end,[87] it must follow that "God to Whom that goodness belongs chiefly, as being substantially possessed, understood and loved, must be the governor of all things." Then follows a series of Scriptural corroborations. Now the greatest goodness among created things is the goodness in the order of the universe which is most perfect, as Aristotle says, and which Scripture confirms in that "God saw all things He had made, and they were very good."[88] The conclusion is "that which is chiefly willed and caused by God is the good consisting in the order of the universe of which He is the cause. Therefore, God, by His intellect and will, governs all things."

Continuing the theme of God's government, Aquinas argues that the nearer a thing is to its cause means that it has the greater share of the effect, and the universe is near to God as its Governor. Furthermore, since earlier, he had shown that "the distinctions and grades among natures" are effects of the Divine Wisdom,[89] hence, "God by His Wisdom governs and rules all things."

Aquinas now turns to the second aspect of Divine Providence, namely, God's preservation of things, in Chapter 65: "Now things are directed to the ultimate end intended by God, namely, the Divine goodness, not only in that they operate, but also in the very fact that they exist." God must stand in relation to the species of things in the same way as in nature the individual generator is related to generation, of which God is *per se* the cause. But in nature, when the generator's action ceases, the generation ceases: hence all species would cease if the Divine operation were to cease. Therefore, by His operation, God preserves things in being.

There are, however, two possible explanations given for the origin of things. One is posited by faith—Creation by God—the other is the view of certain philosophers that things emanated from eternity. Whichever explanation is offered, it is still necessary to affirm that things are preserved in being by God for they last only as long as He wills them to last. Here, Aquinas turns again to Scripture for support, citing: "Upholding all things by His Power" (Hebrews 1:3) and also to Augustine's Commentary on Genesis: ". . . the world would not stand for a single moment if God withdrew His support."[90]

The reason for this is in the following chapters: Chapter 66 makes the fundamental Thomist distinction between God and all creatures—namely, that God's existence and essence are one, while all other beings exist by participation. So whatever brings anything into being does so by God's power. It is developed in Chapter 67: "That in All Things that operate God is the Cause of their Operations." The succeeding Chapter entitled "That God is Everywhere" is claimed to be a necessary inference from the fact, already proven, that God moves all things to their actions. Chapter 69 criticizes Moslem philosophers who deny that God causes the corporeal variations of individual entities.

To have agreed with this view of Averroes would have involved as consequence the denial of providential concern for any individuals, and this is wholly unacceptable to Christianity. Thomas disproved the contention by citing from experience that a hot body produces heat in another body, not coldness, and that the seeds of a man produce only humans. So all effects are caused by God in individuals, but, to avoid confusion,

Thomas is quick to point out in Chapter 71 "That the Divine Providence does not entirely Remove Evil from Things." He had argued earlier[91] that evil was unintentional in the world since all things participate in the goodness of God by imitating God, so evil must be in the lowest order of beings and is essentially privative, that degree of goodness which has hardly any existence at all, for existence is good.

Chapter 70, "How the Same Effect is from God and the Natural Agent" deals with the difficulty of how the same action could be produced by two agents, in this case, both God and man. Aquinas is, of course, eager to preserve the Divine control and at the same time to assert the genuineness of the human freedom of choice. He begins by saying that the power of the lower agent depends on the power of the higher agent, insofar as the higher grants to the lower the power by which it acts, and preserves that power or applies it to action. The same effect is ascribed to a natural agent, not as if God did part and the natural agent also did part, "but as the whole effect proceeds from each, yet in different ways, so the same effect can be ascribed to the instrument as well as to the principal agent." Chapter 71 admits that in what is governed by God may have a defect in the secondary agent, yet without any in God as the first agent, just as there may be a defect in the product of a craftsman, solely because his instrument is defective.

Then Aquinas proceeds to elaborate what has come to be known as the "esthetic argument" used in theodicy for the justification of God. The argument goes approximately thus: perfect goodness in things could not be appreciated unless there were degrees of goodness, so some things have to be better than others. Hence, the chief beauty in things would disappear if the order resulting from distinction and disparity were abolished. In addition, many virtues would vanish unless there were evils for them to overcome or endure. Thus, there would be "no patience of the righteous, if there were no ill-will of the persecutors; nor would there be a place for a vindicating justice if there were no crimes."[92] Aquinas's conclusion is: ". . . it is evident evil deeds, considered as defective, are not from God, but from their defective proximate causes. But so far as they possess activity and entity, they must be from God; even as a limp is from the locomotive power so far as it has movement; but in so far as it has a defect it is from the crookedness of the leg."[93]

Chapter 70 had made the point that Divine Providence does not exclude contingency from things, illustrating this from the fact that even though the sun remains constant, some flowers fail to germinate. Neither does the Divine Providence impose necessity on things.[94] Another consequence is that Providence does not exclude liberty of choice, for if that were the case, it would not have that likeness to God of a voluntary agent, although God's freedom of will is so in a more eminent degree, as proved earlier.[95] Curiously, Chapter 71 insists "that the Divine Providence does not exclude Fortune and Chance," which would seem to derogate from Divine government of the world. This occurs, according to Aquinas, when things happen beyond the intention of an agent, especially if the agent is low in the scale of being, or when there are multiple causes. Chapter 75 insists strongly that the Divine Providence is concerned with singular contingents, "which could only be negatived if God was ignorant of them or uncaring of them," but earlier it was proved that God knows singular things and it cannot be that He lacks the power to care for them, as was also proved earlier, in acknowledging His infinity.[96] St. Thomas concludes this point by citing Matthew 10:29: "Are not two sparrows sold for a farthing: and not one of them shall fall to the ground without your Father . . ." Here our theologian refutes Averroes's erroneous interpretation of Aristotle that Divine providence does not extend to individual things.

Indeed, in Chapter 72 St. Thomas asserts boldly "That God's Providence cares for all individuals immediately." On this issue, the Catholic faith both agrees with and dissents from Plato. It agrees in that it refers universal providence to God, but disagrees with Plato in his denial that every individual thing is subject to Divine providence. Human government fails, says Aquinas, through the ignorance, incompetence and delay of the chief person in charge who cannot know the details of minor matters, but God is not limited in this way. God knows all individual things and does not need labor or time in order to understand them, since in knowing Himself He understands all other things, as shown earlier.[97] Hence, He devises the order of all individuals, and as a result His providence extends to all individuals immediately. Thus, as Romans 13:1 affirms, "Those that are, are ordained of God."

In Chapter 77 Aquinas claims that the execution of Divine providence is accomplished by secondary causes. Essential to the action of Providence are both order and its execution, the former requiring the highest cognitive power, and the latter merely needing the inferior operative power. Thus, it is fitting that the inferior powers should be activated by the higher Divine cognitive power. Chapters 78 and 79 apply the implications: that by means of intellectual creatures less intellectual beings are ruled by God. The higher intellectual creatures are called angels, and their function is to be God's messengers and ministers executing the ordering of Providence.

Chapters 80 and 81 describe the entire hierarchy of beings under the Supreme Being. Chapter 80, making use of both Dionysius's *Concerning the Celestial Hierarchy* and Gregory of Nyssa's Thirty-fourth *Gospel Homily*, covers the hierarchy in descending order from God, with three ranks of angels from the seraphim through the heavenly bodies (planets, stars), down to the lowest rank of spirits who preside over human affairs, and are known as the Principalities. Chapter 81 describes the hierarchy chiefly as it concerns human beings. God is at the highest level, since His Being is His Essence. Immediately below Him are the angels as incorporeal intelligences. Next below them are the weaker, embodied intelligences of humans, who have organs with appetites and will. Their bodily powers are subject to intellect and sense, and execute their orders. Below the humans come the animals, which lack intellectual light but have some knowledge. Below the animals are plants and other creatures devoid of knowledge. Chapter 82 claims that the inferior bodies are ruled by the heavenly bodies.

The summary of all the preceding chapters on Providence is provided in Chapter 83: "we are able to conclude that as regards the design of the order to be imposed on things God governs all things by Himself.[98] . . . As to the execution, however, He governs lower by means of the higher things."

This Aquinas confirms by a citation from St. Augustine *On the Trinity*.[99]

Succeeding Chapters 84 to 87 reject the notion that humans are ruled by the heavenly bodies, and Chapter 88 denies that separate substances can rule humanity, since God alone is in charge of the order of the universe, while Chapter 89 argues that the movement and power of the will is caused by God. In addition, Chapter 90 declares that human power of choice and will are both subject to Divine providence, for the more God loves an object, the more it comes under Divine providence. Therefore, free will is an effect of God's love who then receives spontaneous responses to His Love.

For the preservation of piety Chapters 95 and 96 affirm that the unchangeableness of Divine providence does not exclude the usefulness of prayer, for we do not pray to change Providence (for that is impossible), but that our wish, if good, may be granted. Prevailing prayer must be contemplative, affectionate, humble, and with firm resolution.

God can also work outside the order imposed on things by producing effects without their proximate causes (Chapter 99), yet this is not contrary to nature, just as an artist can modify his art work (Chapter 100); while God alone can work miracles (Chapter 102).

There are obvious difficulties in affirming both God's control of the universe simultaneously with asserting human freedom of choice, and Aquinas tries to meet them in Chapter 104: "Of the Certainty of Divine Providence." Here he insists that if all things are ruled by Providence it seems that nothing is under our own control. In reality, however, our actions are foreseen by God as freely done by us. Nor, St. Thomas adds, can the defectibility of secondary causes by means of which the effects of Providence are produced, deprive Divine providence of certainty, for it belongs to God's Providence sometimes to permit defectible causes to fail, and sometimes to prevent them from failing.

The very important anti-Averroes claim is found in Chapter 113 which asserts that the rational creature is directed in its actions by God, not only in what befits the species, but also in what befits the individual. This is known in experience in that the rational creature is capable of exercising providence and government in relation to others, because of its own knowledge of Divine providence, and these acts are also those of the rational soul capable of perpetuity and as individuals (not merely as a species), since they, too, are directed by Divine providence.

Book IV of the *Summa contra Gentiles*[100] deals with salvation, which is the ultimate purpose of Divine providence. In Chapter 1 in the account of the third type of knowledge to be attained in the hereafter, Aquinas describes how the human mind will be elevated perfectly to gaze upon the things to be revealed, while he prepares the reader for the second type of knowledge, which is that of the mysteries revealed in Scripture and the creeds, such as the Holy Trinity and the Incarnation, and which will only be touched on briefly in passing.

Of the grand mystery of the Incarnation, whereby the Second Person of the Trinity, assumed human nature, St. Thomas says: "The Incarnation of God was the most efficacious assistance to man in his striving for beatitude. All is contained in this most effective help: salvation from despair, the remedy for man's frailty, the remedy for sin, the model for virtue, the assurance of God's friendship; in fact, whatever is needed in the order of knowledge or love by one who tends towards the blessedness of God is contained in this blessed mystery." [101]

On Christ's Resurrection and our future resurrection, St. Thomas declares that as the soul is united to the body, since in its essence it is the form of the body, and the soul was previously proven immortal,[102] therefore, the immortality of souls seems to require the immortality of bodies.

8. Providence in the *Summa Theologiae*

In the *Summa Theologiae* St. Thomas concentrates his teaching on Divine Providence in four articles, which assume the detailed argumentation and conclusions of the consideration of the theme in the earlier *Summa contra Gentiles*. Still these four articles have two advantages over the more extensive treatment in the *Contra Gentiles*. For example, there is a stronger insight into the theodicy by the admirable citation from St. Augustine: "Almighty God would in no way allow evil to exist in His works unless He were so almighty and so good as to produce good even from evil."[103] Also, St. Thomas seems on occasion to provide more apt Scripture for corroboration in the later than the earlier *Summa*. For example, the attribution of providence to God is better confirmed from Ephesians 1:11: "Who worketh all things according to the counsel of His will" than in the roughly translated Romans 13:11 rendered as "Those that are, are ordained by God."[104]

Since there is little point in summarizing a summary, consideration in this section of our chapter will concentrate on three themes related to the Divine providence: Predestination, Election and Reprobation; Sin; and the end and purpose of life as Beatitude and God as its source and sustentation.

Thomas's first article on Predestination simply asks: "Whether men are predestined by God?" The reply itself mentions two of our themes: "*I answer that* it is fitting that God should predestinate men . . . The end towards which created things are disposed by God is two-fold: one which exceeds all proportion and faculty of created nature; and this end is Life Eternal, consisting in the beatific Vision, which is above the nature of every creature. The other end, however, is proportionate to created nature, namely, that the creature must be directed by God, and to destine is to direct or send. Thus is it clear that Predestination as regards its objects is a part of Providence."[105] St. Thomas makes it clear that Predestination as far as God is concerned is active, but as far as its recipients are concerned is wholly passive, for which he cites Romans 8:30: "Whom He predestined, them He also called, and those He called, them He also justified."

Reprobation is defined as a part of God's Providence to permit some to fall away from the end of Eternal Life, and so, "as Providence includes the will to confer grace and glory; so Reprobation includes the will to permit a person to fall into sin, and to impose their punishment of damnation on account of that sin." The important addition is then made "Whence, although anyone reprobated by God cannot acquire grace, nevertheless that he falls into this or that particular sin comes from the use of his free will. Hence it is rightly imputed to him as guilt."[106] This must seem unfair on the part of God; so was

Origen right in declaring that the elect were those whose merits were foreseen by God? St. Thomas will not take this way out to guarantee God's justice at the cost of the sheer generosity and gratuitousness of the gift of salvation, for, he says, this is contradicted by St. Paul in both Titus 3:5 and Romans 9:11-12. Finally, without emphasizing double Predestination, as St. Augustine does, St. Thomas concludes, nevertheless, by citing the latter: "God wills to manifest His goodness in men, in respect to those He predestines by means of His mercy; and in respect to those whom He reprobates by means of his justice." And all must finally be attributed to the inscrutable Divine Will: "Why He chooses some for glory, and reprobates others, has no reason; except the Divine Will." [107]

As to the number of the predestined, Aquinas declares that some say the number will be equal to that of the fallen angels, and yet others say they will be as many as there are angels remaining unfallen. Thomas himself declares that it is better to say, "To God alone is known the number of those for whom eternal happiness is reserved;" but he adds that the number of the elect will probably be a small minority, leaving the reprobates as the vast majority. [108]

As to the cause of evil, St. Thomas agrees with St. Augustine that Good is the only possible source of Evil, since Evil is a privation of goodness. God cannot be charged with the responsibility for evil since He is essentially Being and Goodness and therefore cannot be the cause of tending towards non-being. Furthermore, God cannot be its cause since He is the highest perfection. St. Thomas, as in the *Summa contra Gentiles*, uses the esthetic argument to justify God: "Now the order of the universe requires . . . some things that can and do fail." He also produces a new argument, namely that justice belongs to the order of the universe, and this requires that penalty should be handed out to sinners. "And so God is the author of evil that is penalty, but not of the evil which is fault." [109]

We shall conclude with the briefest consideration of the Beatitude of God which is the end of Divine Providence for humanity and which is a final communication of God's Blessedness. In answering the question, "Whether all other Beatitude is included in the Beatitude of God?" St. Thomas replies seraphically: "*I answer that*: Whatever is desirable in whatsoever beatitude . . . pre-exists wholly and in an eminent degree in the Divine Beatitude. As to contemplative happiness, God possesses a continual and most certain contemplation of Himself and of all things else; as to that which is active He has the governance of the whole universe. As to earthly happiness, which consists in pleasure, riches, power, dignity and fame, He possesses, according to Boethius, joy in Himself and all things else for His delectation; instead of riches, He has that complete self-sufficiency which is promised by riches; in place of power, He has omnipotence; for dignities, the government of all things; and in place of fame, he possesses the admiration of the whole universe."[110]

In this single citation are exhibited several of St. Thomas's qualities as a writer and thinker: the capacity to make abstraction concrete by analogies which also indicate the transcendental nature of God; an existential concern for ultimate human happiness; the luminous lucidity of expression like sunshine in a cloudless sky; a devotion to God as is His due; and, for our present purpose, an indication of how far the Divine providence extends, even to Eternity!

9. A Final Critique

Much as St. Thomas deserves to be admired, criticisms of his philosophical theology have been made from time to time, which should be mentioned before a positive, concluding evaluation of his work is made. His 'Five Ways' or demonstrations of the existence of God have been attacked on several grounds. It can be argued that to assume to prove the existence of an admittedly transcendent Being by the categories derived from common human empirical experience is unacceptable. For example, Victor Preller argues that if the proposition that any efficient cause of motion must precede its effect in time (and presumably contiguous in space) is to be taken seriously it "automatically excludes the introduction of a nontemporary, nonspatial first mover who moves by means of efficient causality."[111] Preller adds that "Aquinas's position is deceptively simple. His most profound 'reasons' for asserting the existence of God are 'throw aways'—laconic claims made in contexts other than the five ways. Basically, they can be reduced to the optimistic claim that no natural inclination of the human will can be *inane*. There must be in reality something that is able to give rest to the frustrated love and intellectual appetite of man."[112] The difficulty is that the use of meta-empirical language is ultimately invalid for humans living and thinking in the empirical world and expressing thoughts through the senses, and God cannot be conceived by humans, except negatively or with the shadows of the analogical approach.[113]

Other serious criticisms of Aquinas's thought include the extraordinary fact that in the *Summa Theologiae* he postpones any consideration of the historical understanding of God in Christ until long after the discussion of the nature of Grace. As Per Erik Persson points out, Aquinas cannot easily fit historical revelation into his philosophical framework, and in consequence "conceives the necessity of grace from the standpoint of how man's metaphysically appointed nature is to be defined. What is said on the biblical revelation of sin and the Fall is merely a supplementary disclosure which essentially changes nothing in the existing scheme of things."[114]

There are also other weaknesses which Aquinas shares with Augustine, and in some cases with Calvin too. The "esthetic argument" for example rationalizes evil far too easily and largely absolves the Creator, while the notion that evil is merely absence or privation of good utterly fails to do justice to the horrific and destructive dimensions of sin and evil. Further, while Thomas does not emphasize double Predestination, as Augustine did, he cannot rid the doctrine of unfairness and takes unworthy refuge in asserting that the just will of God is inscrutable, and that all deserve damnation but the elect are saved by the clemency of God. In addition, while Thomas in his doctrine of Providence allows for the positive and negative effects of secondary causes, he has not overcome the basic difficulty of correlating Divine omniscience and omnipotence with a genuine human freedom of choice.

Finally, there is much that is impressive in the doctrine of Providence as interpreted by St. Thomas, as in his philosophical theology as a whole. His doctrine of Providence interprets God as vigilant in the marvelous ordering of the universe by His will, in the variety of creatures inhabiting the world, in a related and dependent hierarchy, as in its constancy and consistency for the most part. This doctrine also sees God as the first efficient cause, the exemplary cause, and the final cause, who shares His perfections with many creatures, whom He creates and sustains. He perceives God as planning for His undeserving human creatures a life of grace leading to final blessedness in the after-life, and a Mediator in Christ Who as God-man is the Way, the Truth and the Life, and Who provides in the Church, His Body, a community of pilgrims in *via*, also a round of Sacraments that hallow every stage of human life from Baptism to the *Viaticum*, with the perpetual benefits of the Eucharist. This is his deep and wide interpretation of the term "Providence"–in which God creates and provides for His adopted children with whom He shares such perfections as reason, will, love and holiness forever. St. Thomas was, moreover, an impressive witness to Providence as an admirable commender of the Christian faith in his lectures, books, sermons, and exemplary life, and a brilliant defender of it against its intellectual critics and detractors.

Etienne Gilson, an outstanding modern interpreter, sums it up: "His thought has tried to express in rational language the whole destiny of the Christian, but, in reminding him often that he has in this life to follow a path of exile without light or horizon, he never ceased to direct his steps towards those heights whence he can descry, rising out of the haze of the distance, the confines of the Promised Land."[115] Using a similar image of climbing, J. H. Walgrave stresses the humility of Aquinas: "Thomas Aquinas does not climb the mountain to have it under his feet. He only climbs the hills round the mountain and from these he looks to the unapproachable clouded mountain peak, and he kneels down in the only possible attitude of faith:

adoro te devote
latens deitas (115)

He was, doubtless, the greatest theologian of the Middle Ages who is still widely read for his relevance today. One must admire the discipline of his *magnum opus*, the *Summa Theologiae*, in which he started each topic with the three strongest arguments he could muster against the position he wished to defend. His philosophical theology represents at one and the same time a profound respect for human reason, while acknowledging reason's consummation in faith, and nature's completion in grace. It is a great privilege, metaphorically, to have sat at his feet in Paris, Cologne, Naples and Rome.

Notes

1 Among others, see P. Mandonnet, *Siger de Brabant et l'averroisme latine du XIIIe siècle in Les philosophes belges, Textes et Etudes* (Vols. VI-VII, 1908, 1911) published by the Institute of Philosophy of the University of Louvain; F. Van Steenberghen, *Siger dans l'histoire de l'aristotelisme* in *Les philosophes belges, Textes et Etudes* (Vol. XIII, 1942); Eds. G. Verbeke and D. Verhelst, *Aquinas and the Problems of His Time* (Leuven University Press and the Hague: Nijhoff) for articles "La connaissance que Thomas d'Aquin put avoir du Monde Islamique" and "St. Thomas, Averroes et l'Averroisme"; also David Burrell, *Knowing the Unknowable God. Ibn-Sina, Maimonides, Aquinas* (South Bend, Indiana: Notre Dame University Press, 1986).

2 Jacques Maritain, *The Angelic Doctor. The Life and Thought of Saint Thomas Aquinas* (New York: The Dial Press, 1931), pp. 248-49, citing Leo III's Encyclical and on p. 276 referring to Pius IX's Encyclical. For the diminished reputation of St. Thomas since Vatican II, see Anthony Kenny, *Aquinas* (New York: Hill and Wang, 1980), p. 28.

3 *Op. cit.*, preface, p. ix.

4 *Op. cit.*, p. 143.

5 See Per Erik Persson, *Sacra Doctrina. Reason and Revelation in Aquinas* (Philadelphia: Fortress Press, 1970), p. 13, which also refers to the *Codex iuris canonici*, canon 1366, sect. 2.

6 *Thomas Aquinas* by M. C. D'Arcy, S. J., (London: Ernest Benn, Ltd., 1930), p. 252.

7 These included commentaries on Isaiah, Jeremiah, Lamentations, the Psalms, the Book of Job, the Gospels of Matthew and John, and the Epistles of St. Paul.

8 They were 48 in all and of which 13 are possibly but not certainly his. The more important among them are the following: *De Ente et essentia* (On Being and Essence); *De intellectu unitate* [contra Averroistas] (On the unity of the intellect [against the Averroist]); *De aeternitate mundi [contra murmurantes]* (On the eternity of the world [against the murmurers]); *Compendium theologiae [ad fratrem Reginaldum]* (A compend of theology [for Brother Reginald]); *De perfectione vitae spiritualis* (On the perfection

of the spiritual life); (*Contra errores Graecorum) [ad Urbanum IV Pontificem].*

(Against the errors of the Greeks) [for Urban IV, Supreme Pontiff]; *Collationes de Credo in Deum [Devotissima expositio super symbolum]* (A most devout Exposition of the Apostles' Creed); and, finally, *Officium corporis Christ [Officium de festo Corporis Christi] [ad mandatum Urbani Papae IV]* (Office of the Feast of the Body of Christ on the mandate of Pope Urban IV).

Accounts of the different genres in which Aquinas wrote can be found in M.-D. Chenu, *op. cit.*, chs. VI-XII, and for an evaluation of the authenticity of the opuscules see I. T. Eschmann, *A Catalogue of St. Thomas's Work* which is published as an appendix in E. Gilson, *The Christian Philosophy of Saint Thomas* (New York: Random House, 1956), pp. 379-439.

9 M.-D. Chenu, O. P., *Toward Understanding Saint Thomas* (Chicago: Henry Regnery Co., 1965), p. 285.

10 *Summa contra Gentiles* (henceforth abbreviated to S.C.G., 1, 7). There is an admirably full and careful treatment of *Reason and Revelation in Aquinas,* which is the sub-title of the book authored by Per Erik Persson, and the main title of which is *Sacra Doctrina*, trans. Ross Mackenzie (Philadelphia: Fortress Press and Oxford: Basil Blackwell, 1970).

11 *The Philosophy of St. Thomas Aquinas* (Cambridge: Heffer and Sons, 1928), p. 281. On the same theme Maritain adds: "Let us say that the sanctity of St. Thomas is the sanctity of the mind." (*Angelic Doctor*, p. 116).

12 See James A. Weisheipl, O. P., for an excellent biography of Aquinas which distinguishes carefully between legend and history. The book is *Friar Thomas D'Aquino* (Garden City, New York: Doubleday, 1974). The abduction and attempted seduction are reported and discussed on pp. 26-36.

13 See Maritain's *Angelic Doctor*, pp. 40-41.

14 Cited p. 89 of M.-D. Chenu, *Towards Understanding St. Thomas*, whose authority is the *Acta Sanctorum*, March 7, *Processus inquisitionis*, c. 9, n. 77, 712; Foster ed. 107-8.

15 See M. Grabmann, "Magister Petrus von Hibernia, der Jugendlehrer des Thomas von Aquin" in *Mittelalterliches Geistesleben. Abhandlugen zur Geschichte der Scholastik und Mystik* (Munich, 1926) I, pp. 249-65. Translations of Arabic philosophers were undertaken by Michael the Scot, the favorite court philosopher of Emperor Frederick II in Naples, and also, on the recommendation of Aquinas, by William of Moerbeke. For the former see R. deVaux, "La première entrée d'Averroes chez les Latins,"

Revue des sciences philosophiques et théologiques (Paris, 1933), XXII, pp. 193-245; for the latter, see M. DeWolf, *Histoire de la philosophie mediévale*, 6th edn., II (Louvain-Paris, 1936), pp. 44-56.

16 Weisheipl, *Friar Thomas of Aquino*, p. 4.

17 For a summary of the doctrinal elements involved in the struggle between St. Thomas and the Augustinians, as well as a bibliography, see L. Gilson's "Signification historique de la théologie de saint Thomas," which is part of a longer article, "Thomas d'Aquin" in the *Dictionnaire de théologie catholique* (Paris, 1946), XV, I, col. 651-693.

18 On the founding of the Order of Preachers and the need for it in the Catholic Church in the early thirteenth century, see P. Mandonnet, *Saint Dominique, L'idée, l'homme, et l'oeuvre* (Paris, 1938), especially II, pp. 83f.

19 The traditional story is recounted by Anthony Kenny, *Aquinas*, pp. 2-3. The shorter and likelier, but less attractive account appears in Weisheipl, *Friar Thomas D'Aquino*, p. 44, with the attribution to William of Tocco, *Hystoria*, ch. 12. Fr. Weisheipl aptly remarks that the taunt "sums up the two well-known features of Thomas, his large physique and the constant reserve he had cultivated since adolescence." (*Ibid.*)

20 Cf. A. Wilmart, "La tradition littéraire et textuelle de *l'Adoro te devote," in Recherches de théologie ancienne et mediévale* (Louvain: Abbé de Mont César), I (1929), pp. 21-40; 146-176. For the religious poetry of Aquinas as a whole, see F. J. Raby, *Thomas Aquinas and the Poetry of the Eucharist* (Oxford: Clarendon Press, 1927), and W. J. Ong, "Wit and Mystery: A Revaluation in Mediaeval Latin Hymnody" in *Speculum: A Journal of Mediaeval Studies* (Cambridge, Mass.), XXII (1947), pp. 402-411.

21 This work, meaning *Against the Errors of the Greeks*, was requested by Urban IV, formerly Patriarch of Jerusalem, who had been approached by the newly victorious Michael Paleologos, the emperor, who was menaced by the Muslims, and who hoped that the schism of East and West might be mended. The Pope asked Aquinas to provide a theological critique of an anti-Greek anthology of texts which had recently arrived from the East. (M.-D. Chenu, *Toward Understanding St. Thomas*, pp. 343-4.)

22 This is a continuous commentary on the four Gospels chiefly by means of texts taken from the Fathers.

23 The enumeration is found in Jacques Maritain, *The Angelic Doctor*, p. 62.

24 For an overall view of this complicated and still controversial matter involving Aquinas's use of different Arabic, Jewish, and Latin translations of and commentaries on Aristotle, see M. -D. Chenu, *op. cit.*, ch. VI, pp. 203-232. For a brief account of Averroism, see J. van Steenberghen, transl. from the French by L. Johnson, *Aristotle in the West. The Origins of*

Latin Aristotelianism (Louvain: 1955), pp. 198-235. This author holds that four of the tenets of Averroes were dangerous to the Christian religion: the denial of Providence, the eternity of the world, the unity of the intellect, and the suppression of human freedom. See Steenberghen, *Siger dans l'histoire de l'Aristotelisme* (Louvain, 1942), p. 495.

25 Siger changed, according to Chenu (*op. cit.*, p. 338) and was "tossed from provocative Averroism to objective Aristotelianism."

26 See E. Gilson, "Boece de Dacie et la double vérité" in *Archives d'histoire doctrinale et litteraire du moyen age*, XXII (1955), pp. 81-89.

27 Anthony Kenny, *Aquinas*, p. 18, who also points out that the theory of a single common intellect is doubtfully attributed to Aristotle, but that the Greek philosopher undoubtedly affirmed the eternity of the world.

28 Weisheipl, *Friar Thomas D'Aquino*, p. 320, who also adds: "Something had to give way after five years of driving himself day in and day out" (*Ibid.*) (on the *Summa* and Commentaries on Aristotle's works). The sources for the breakdown are Bartholomew of Capua, a prominent layman in royal service, who, presumably, like Thomas's first biographer, William of Tocco, derived his information from Thomas's brother Dominican (*socius*), Reginald, who completed the *Summa* with supplements from other works of Thomas Aquinas. It is also important to recognize that the commentaries on Aristotle's *Physics, Metaphysics, Ethics* and *Politics*, were all written after the year 1268.

29 M. C. D'Arcy, *Thomas Aquinas*, p. 3.

30 M.-D. Chenu, *op. cit.*, pp. 13-14.

31 The *Summa Theologiae*, 1, 3, prologue, henceforth abbreviated to S.T., as the *Summa Contra Gentiles* will be abbreviated to S.C.G., and the *Compendium Theologiae* will be abbreviated to Comp. theol.

32 S.C.G. I, 18 and *Comp. theol.* I, 19.

33 S.C.G. I, 16.

34 S.C.G. I, 20; S.T. I, 3, 3, *ad Resp.*

35 S.C.G. I, 21; S.T. I, 3, 3, *ad Resp.*

36 S.T. I, 3, 6, *ad Resp.*

37 S.C.G. I, 35.

38 E. Gilson, *The Philosophy of St. Thomas Aquinas* (trans. from *Le Thomisme*, 3rd rev. edn. by E. Bullough; Cambridge, England: Heffer & Sons, 1924), p. 87.

39 S.T. I, 13, 3.

40 F. C. Copleston, *Aquinas* (Harmondsworth and Baltimore: Penguin Books, 1955), p. 131.

41 *In librum De Causis*, lectio 6, cited Copleston, *op. cit.*, p. 132.

42 S.C.G. I, 37 and S.T. I, 6, 1, *ad Resp.*

43 S.C.G. I, 43 and S.T. I, 7, 1, *ad Resp.*

44 S.C.G. I, 65 and S.T. I, 14, 2, *ad Resp.*

45 God knows, and from this we can argue that He wills, since both are perfections shared in a lesser degree by humans, God's creatures (S.C.G. I, 72); Gilson in *The Philosophy of St. Thomas Aquinas*, asserts of St. Thomas's teaching: "To deny to God the knowledge of future contingents is tantamount to render Providence impossible" and in denying this denial he was confuting Averroes. Of course, in the strict sense God does not see ahead (etymologically "providet"), being above time, He sees all events at once, not in temporal succession.

46 Copleston, *op. cit.*, p. 107.

47 S.T. I, 2, 1 *sed contra.*

48 *De Fide Orthodoxa*, 3, to be found in *Patrologia Graeca* XCIV, col. 795.

49 S.C.G. I, 13 and 11, 16 *ad Amplius.*

50 S.T. I, 2, 3, *sed Resp.*

51 *Op. cit.*, p. 73.

52 Etienne Gilson, *The Christian Philosophy of St. Thomas Aquinas* (New York: Random House, 1956), p. 92.

53 S.T. I, 75, 2 *ad* 1.

54 Copleston, *op. cit.*, p. 54.

55 Copleston, *op. cit.*, pp. 125-126.

56 Anthony Kenny, *The Five Ways, St. Thomas's Proofs of God's Existence* (London: Routledge & Kegan Paul, 1969). To take only two examples, he declares of the fourth way, with some disdain: "The notion of *Ipsum Esse Subsistens*, therefore, so far from being a profound metaphysical analysis of the divine nature, turns out to be the Platonic idea of a predicate which is at best uninformative and at worst unintelligible." (p. 95) And of the fifth way he observes that if irregular adaptive behaviour is a characteristic of intelligence for humans, why look beyond humans for

its explanation, and if regular adaptive behaviour is an index of intelligence "then Aquinas has given no reason why we should not call the swallows and the spiders intelligent themselves, rather than looking for an intelligence to direct them from outside the universe." (p. 119)

57 The term "natural theology" is used pejoratively by Aquinas to refer to three kinds of superstitution, the fables that make up the theology of poets, the civil theology of the State, and physical theology. This is pointed out by J. H. Walgrave in his article, "The use of philosophy in the theology of St. Thomas Aquinas," contained in eds. Verbecke & Verhelst, *Aquinas and the Problems of His Time* (Leuven: University Press and The Hague: Nijhoff, 1976), p. 184.

58 This paragraph is a summary of the opening of Victor J. Preller's innovative study, *Divine Science and the Science of God* (Princeton: Princeton University Press, 1967), p. 3. Its sub-title is significant: "A Reformulation of Thomas Aquinas."

59 S.T. II-II, 94, 1.

60 See the following paradoxical explanation of the positive value of the negative knowledge of God in metaphysical analysis: *Vel potest dici quod hoc ipsum quod scimus de Deo quid non est, supplet in divina scientia locum cognitionis quid est.* (Aquinas's Commentary on the Trinity of Boethius.)

61 J. H. Walgrave's article (*op. cit.*, pp. 184-86) has proved useful in making this series of contrasts. The Source in Aquinas to which this sentence is attached can be found in S.T. I, 8.

62 This theme is finely expounded throughout P. E. Persson, *Sacra Doctrina. Reason and Revelation in Aquinas.*

63 S.T. I, q. 8.

64 *Commentary on the Trinity of Boethius,* 3, 1, *ad* 3.

65 S.T. I, 1, *respondeo.*

66 *Ibid.*

67 *Sacra Doctrina*, p. 296.

68 M.-D. Chenu, *op. cit.*, p. 226, note 45.

69 *Ibid.*, note 46.

70 *De Causis*, lect. 6. The Gilson reference is to "L'esprit de la philosophie mediévale", 2nd edn., in *Etudes de philosophie mediévale*, XXXIII (1944), p. 94, note 5.

71 S.T. I, 19, 2, *ad Resp.*

72 S.T. I, 108, 5, *ad* 4 and S.C.G. III, 80.

73 S.T. I, 50, 1 *ad Resp.*

74 S.T. I, 75, 7 *ad* 3.

75 S.T. I, 76, 8 *ad Resp.*; S.T. I, 118, 3 *ad Resp.*

76 S.T. I, 77, 2, *ad Resp.*

77 *De Anima*, 1, 4, *ad Resp.*

78 *Ibid.*

79 S.T. I-II, 4, 6, *ad Resp.*

80 S.T. I-II, 4, 8, *ad Resp.*

81 Bk. II, ch. 4.

82 *Toward Understanding St. Thomas*, p. 304. This structure has, however, been criticized by A. Hayen, *Saint Thomas d'Aquin et la Vie de l'Eglise*, Essais philosophiques 6 (Louvain and Paris), pp. 88f. who disagrees with Chenu, pointing out that while Thomas accepted Neo-Platonic emanationism in his Commentary on the Sentences, he preferred a "theological realism" in the *Summa Theologiae*, and he proposes that Thomas's design is more accurately rendered as "Part I: God as Being, Part II:9 God as End."

83 S.T. I, 2, prologue to article 1.

84 In dealing with the *Summa contra Gentiles* use will be made of Anton C. Pégis's annotated edition of Vol. II of *The Basic Writings of St. Thomas Aquinas* (New York: Random House, 1945).

85 S.C.G., Bk. II, 4.

86 S.C.G., Bk. III, 20.

87 S.C.G., Bk. III, 17.

88 Genesis, 1:3.

89 S.C.G., Bk. II, 45.

90 *De Genesi ad Litt.*, IV, 12 (P.L. 34, 304).

91 S.C.G., Bk. III, 47.

92 S.C.G., Bk. III, 71. The esthetic argument is on pp. 130-131 in Pegis, *Basic Writings*, II.

93 *Op. cit.*, p. 132.

94 Bk. I, 88 insists that creatures have a likeness to God without which it would be a deprivation.

95 S.C.G., Bk. I, 65.

96 S.C G., Bk. II, 22.

97 S.C.G., Bk. I, 46.

98 As proved in S.C.G., III, 77.

99 Augustine, *De Trinitate*, III, 4 (P.L. 42, 873).

100 In the citations from Bk. IV of the *Summa contra Gentiles*, use has been made of Charles J. O'Neil's vigorous translation, entitled *On the Truth of the Catholic Faith* (Garden City, N.Y.: Hanover House, 1957), and the reference to the citation is IV, 1, para. 5.

101 S.C.G., IV, 55, para. 7.

102 S.C.G., II, 4.

103 Augustine, *Enchiridion*, XI (P.L. 40, 236) and S.T. I, 22, 2 should be compared with S.C.G., III, 71.

104 Compare S.T. I, 22, 2 with S.G.C., III, 86.

105 S.T., I, 21, 1.

106 S.T., I, 23, 3.

107 S.T., I, 23, 5.

108 S.T., I, 23, 7.

109 S.T., I, 49, 2.

110 S.T., I, 26, 4. Further, it is important to note that Beatitude has two meanings for St. Thomas. In the first case God is the Uncreated Good whose infinite goodness alone is able to satisfy perfectly the will of man; and, secondly, the enjoyment that cannot be found in this life, but only in the full view of the essence of God in the life to come. (S.T. I, 12, 1; I-II, 3, 8, *ad Resp.*)

111 Victor J. Preller, *Divine Science and the Science of God*, p. 117.

112 Preller, *op. cit.*, p. 156f.

113 Persson, *Sacra Doctrina*, pp. 175-6.

114 *The Philosophy of St. Thomas Aquinas*, p. 281.

115 Walgrave's essay in Eds. G. Verbeke and D. Verhelst, *Aquinas and the Problems of His Time* (Leuven: University Press and The Hague: Nijhoff, 1976), p. 193. The citation can be literally translated thus:

"I adore you devoutly
Hidden Deity."

Chapter 4

Calvin's Doctrine of Providence

Both Augustine and Aquinas had a very high regard for Scripture as the Wisdom of God, but, they were also strongly influenced by the dominant philosophies of their day and related their theologies respectively to Neo-Platonism and Aristotelianism. Calvin by contrast, though learned in the Fathers, and greatly indebted to Augustine, was first, foremost, and last, a *biblical* theologian, and not a philosophical theologian. No one deserves this description more than he, with the possible exception of Karl Barth. Patrologist and humanist as Calvin was, and man of great intelligence and faith, his determination was to hew to the biblical line, and he expected his writing and preaching to be tested by the biblical criterion. He wrote:

> Let this then be a settled principle, that there is no Word of God to which place should be given in the Church save that which is contained, first in the Law and Prophets, and secondly in the writings of the Apostles, and that the only right method of teaching in the Church is according to the prescription and rule of the Word. [1]

1. The Primacy of Scripture

He recognized, however, that the Scripture is no more than a historic document unless the Holy Spirit uses the biblical writings to put us in contact with the Word of God, and enables us to discover this as God's Word as well as to accept it for our spiritual illumination. Calvin insists:

> For as God alone is a fit witness of Himself in his Word, so also the Word will not find acceptance in men's hearts before it is sealed by the inward testimony of the Spirit. The same Spirit, therefore, who has spoken through the mouths of the prophets must penetrate into our hearts to persuade us that they faithfully proclaimed what had been divinely commanded. [2]

Now this does not mean that Calvin, while believing in the Divine inspiration of the Bible, teaches its literal inspiration. On the contrary, although the Scripture is an instrument by means of which the Lord provides the illumination of the Spirit for the faithful, "but it is not identifiable with the Lord himself . . . The authors of the biblical books wrote under the inspiration of the Holy Spirit; nonetheless, they were able to introduce into it human errors on points of detail which do not affect its teaching."[3] T.H.L. Parker, a careful commentator on Calvin's own biblical commentaries, sums up the situation well in saying that Calvin "often speaks in such a way as to make it appear that the human writers of Scripture are virtually unthinking stenographers, writing at the verbal dictation of the Holy Spirit. On the other hand, he is alive to differences of style and outlook between Biblical authors, and to minor discrepancies between one part of Scripture and another."[4]

In the 1539 edition of *The Institutes* Calvin gave relatively little consideration to the doctrine of Providence, but this was rectified in the 1559 edition. It appears that Calvin was anxious to avoid any impression that God might be envisaged deistically, that is, that after Creation He left the world and its inhabitants to go their own way. In his definitive edition of 1559, as if regretting his earlier brevity in Book I, xvi-xvii, he devoted two chapters to providence, and, what can be regarded as a particular application of providence, namely predestination, is separately treated also in four chapters as part of the redemptive work of the Holy Spirit in Book III, xxi-xxiv. These facts of themselves show the central and increasing importance of Providence in Calvin's theology.[5] His denial of a deistic God is contained in the statement:

> Moreover, to make God a momentary Creator, who once for all finished, would be cold and barren, and we must differ from profane men especially in that we see the presence of divine power shining as much in the continuing state of the universe as in its inception.[6]

At the very outset Calvin is anxious that his readers should acknowledge that God, far from being an observer of earth from heaven, is the governor of all events as well as of all individuals high and low in the social order.[7] God provides the order of the world whereby night follows day, winter follows summer, months succeed months and years, and even in the modifications and exceptions to these regularities, He reminds us of his existence and of our dependence upon Him. This is God's general Providence which takes care of all living things, and, according to Richard Stauffer, God is known in his Providence as both omniscient and omnipotent, as seen in the preaching of Calvin even more strongly than in *The Institutes*.[8] In consequence, God knows every event before it happens, whether great or small in history and in the lives of individuals. In addition, Providence consists in the fact that the Creator, not content to be omniscient, conducts and governs all things with power.

Calvin's Biblical sources for general providence are Psalms 104 and 115, which assert that God feeds all living creatures; Proverbs 19, which affirms that God overrules the plans of men; Jeremiah 10, which claims that God is "King of the nations"; Matthew 10:29, the passage that claims men are much more important than sparrows, yet God takes care of the birds; and Acts 17 in Paul's sermon in Athens, citing Aratus, that "In Him we live and move and have our beings." Calvin's 33rd Sermon on the Book of Daniel sums up God's omnipotence thus: "See therefore how God does not merely observe from heaven what happens here below, but He controls all things with his hand and his strength and leads them to the end which He has ordered in his deliberation, which nothing can dispose except according to his will."[9] Calvin in his doctrine of Providence has three foes in mind: not only the Deists, but also those who affirm that what happens is mere contingency and chance or the goddess luck (*fortuna*) and the stoics who believe in a predetermined fate. He is convinced that God is continuously creating (*creatio continuata*) and permanently in control. To use terms made familiar by Calvin's theological successors in the Reformed Church, there are three aspects of Providence: *creatio* (creation), *sustentatio* (preservation), and *gubernatio* (government or overruling).

In characteristic fashion, Calvin supports his conviction of God's constant overruling by Biblical references; in particular, to Christ's declaration that He and the Father are always at work (John 5:17), to Paul's teaching at Athens that "in Him we live, move, and have our being", and to the instruction of the Epistle of the Hebrews (1:3) that all things are sustained by Christ "who upholds the universe."[10]

In 1545 Calvin supplemented what he had written in previous editions of *The Institutes* in his treatise *Against the Libertines.* Here he separated Providence into three different but complementary aspects. First, he referred to "the order of nature" according to which God directs all creatures according to the condition and character which He gave each in creating them, and this was in conformity with the laws which God had determined in His universal operation. But, in contrast, God has also a special providence by which He operates on his creatures making them serve his good will and his justice, by which constant intervention He helps his servants, at one time punishing the wicked, at another testing the patience of his faithful ones, or paternally chastising them. All this is a series of external influences on humanity. But, in the third aspect of Providence, God intervenes constantly in the interior life of the faithful: thus He "governs the faithful, living and reigning in them by his Holy Spirit". Here, as Wendel says, one can rightly recognize "salutary grace."[11]

An even clearer demarcation of the spheres of Divine Providence is his fourfold delineation of it in *A Defence of the Secret Providence of God by which He executes His Eternal Decrees* (1558). There is first God's General Providence in which He is demonstrated as Creator and Ruler of all things; second, God's Special Providence for all creatures; third, God's Providential care of all Humanity; fourthly and finally, God's Providential Care of the Church in which He demonstrates that He is the Father of His family.

2. A Pastoral Concern for Providence

Furthermore, Calvin asserts that "every success is God's blessing, and calamity and adversity [are] his curse."[12] The more one studies Calvin's doctrine of Providence, the clearer it becomes that his interest in it is not so much theoretical or philosophical, as wholly pastoral. Hence, the heading of the second chapter on Providence (I, xvii) is "HOW WE MAY APPLY THIS DOCTRINE TO OUR BENEFIT." He begins the chapter by asserting three things: God's Providence applies to the future as well as to the past; as the determinative principle of all things it sometimes works through an intermediary, sometimes without, and sometimes contrary to every intermediary; and, thirdly, he strives to show God's concern for the whole human race, and, particularly His vigilance in ruling the Church.[13] Calvin warns that the causes of many events are hidden and that it sometimes looks "as if God were making sport of men by throwing them about like balls." [14]

He insists that God has the best reasons for his plan and this is "either to instruct his own people in patience, or to correct their wicked affections and tame their lust, or to subjugate them to self-denial, or to arouse them from sluggishness; again, to bring low the proud, to shatter the cunning of the impious, and to overthrow their devices."[15] Clearly, this declaration not only explains the difficulties the godly meet, but is a veritable cordial of confidence and encouragement for the faithful.

Calvin was never tired of insisting that God's ways transcend the human capacity to unravel them–they are an abyss in which we enter with danger, and this recognition should humble our proud, interrogating spirits. He cites Paul with approval: "O the depths of the riches and wisdom and knowledge of God! How unsearchable are his judgments and how inscrutable his ways!" (Romans 11:23-24).[16] Similarly, Calvin affirms the sublimity of God as celebrated by Job: "For after the author, in surveying above and below the frame of the universe, has magnificently discoursed concerning God's works, he finally adds: 'Behold! these are but the outskirts of his ways, and how small a thing is heard therein!'" (Job 26:14).[17] From this citation Calvin draws the conclusion that there is an important distinction "between the wisdom that resides with God and the portion of wisdom God has prescribed for men."[18] Again, the appositeness of his Biblical citations is impressive, as is the implication that the appropriate response is that of the reverent trust of Providence.

While asserting Divine control, the Reformer also insists that God's Providence does not relieve men from responsibility or excuse them from exercising proper prudence, nor exculpate their wickedness.[19] Belief in God's overruling Providence is a profound source of solace to believers, resulting in "Gratitude of mind for the favorable outcome of things, patience in adversity, and also incredible freedom from worry about the future all necessarily follow from this knowledge."[20] Furthermore, being sure of God's Providence is security in all adversities, as Joseph knew in forgetting the treachery of his brothers, and, turning his thoughts to God, he forgot the injustice and even comforted his brothers.[21] But even while they recognize the hand of God in events, the faithful will not overlook secondary causes, either for gratitude to those who have been kind to them, or neglect to consign justice deserved by the malevolent, even though both, in different ways, are agents of God. Thus, remembering the certainty of Providence, our hearts are filled with joyful trust in God.[22]

Calvin also tries to meet the objection that God is said "to repent" in Scripture, as implying ignorance or inconstancy on His part, and presumably uncertainty in the Divine government of the world.[23] The examples given of the use of this term in the Bible are Genesis 6:6, I Samuel 15:11, Jeremiah 18:8, and Isaiah 38:1, 5. Calvin insists that this usage is not literal, but figurative, an anthropomorphic and accommodating way of speaking about God. This, he insists, is conclusively shown in I Samuel 15:29, where it is said of God: "the Glory of Israel will not lie or repent, for He is not a man, that He should repent." [24]

In his preliminary exposition of Providence Calvin affirms that God uses the works of the ungodly to execute His judgments, but that He remains unsullied. We may remark here that Calvin is unwilling to make use of Augustine's escape-hatch, namely, that God *permits* evil rather than wills it.[25] Scripture, Calvin insists, clearly records that God hardened Pharaoh's heart, and according to Luke, "the whole church says that Herod and Pilate conspired to do what God's hand and plan had decreed [Acts 4:28]. And, indeed, unless Christ had been crucified according to God's will, where would we have redemption?"[26] Moreover, God will allow evil to be committed, only because, being almighty, He can make good come out of evil. Calvin finally says that Augustine's answer will satisfy modest minds, which he then quotes: "Since the Father delivered up the Son, and Christ, his body, and Judas his Lord, why in this delivering up is God just and man guilty, unless because in the one thing they have done, the cause of their doing is not one?"[27]

Having followed Calvin's doctrine of Providence in the two chapters of the first Book of *The Institutes* of 1559, we must seek for further information on his instruction in his homiletical works, as we did in the case of Augustine. God's paternal care maintains not only believers, but also unbelievers, and, amusingly, the Reformer declares that even the wicked drink and eat and God generously nourishes them, even though often they are much fatter than believers![28]

In His Providence God is also the master of history, and empires rise and fall at His determination, whether that of Assyria, or that of the Medes and Persians, and that of Rome, and He decides whether military engagements shall issue in victory or defeat.[29] Hence, Providence is expressive not only of Divine power, but also of Divine justice. This is not to be known by human observation: the conviction is born of faith, and even more is it founded upon hope. As Richard Stauffer reminds us, Calvin's sermons more than once underline the eschatological dimensions of a true understanding of Providence.[30]

Since God makes use of human beings as His agents in Providence by their concurrence with His will, human passivity supposedly due to fatalism is absolutely forbidden, and so is any lack of appreciation for God's benevolent human agents. Also, since God governs all individuals, as well as societies, even social differences between individuals are not a matter of chance. Calvin preached thus: "Don't attribute it to luck when we see one person will be rich and another poor: but let us acknowledge that God has arranged it thus, and not without reason. It is true that we do not always see why God should have enriched one and left another in poverty. We cannot have a certain understanding about that; and therefore God wishes us often to lower our eyes in order to do Him the honor of affirming that He governs men by His will and according to His counsel which is incomprehensible to us."[31]

According to the Reformer even the turbulent, apparently dysteleological and clearly disquieting events of special Providence that befall the believers have to be accepted by them as a power ordained by God mysteriously for their good. Nor do the wicked and unbelievers escape from the power of Providence, for otherwise the world would be in a state of complete ruin, for they would, if unrestrained by God, destroy the believers and cause the name of God to be condemned to total oblivion.

Inevitably, Calvin had to consider the question: why did God allow the wicked to trouble the world? Calvin's sermons, according to Stauffer, offer three responses. One is that God allows the existence and manifestation of evil so that Satan's minions will condemn themselves to a deserved death by their actions, an argument that anticipates the negative side of Predestination. A second answer is that evil as willed by God is the just judgment that God exercises towards humanity. The third and most frequently used response is that evil can be conceived as a power in the redemptive plan of God. Like unruly children who do not respond to the testimonies of their father's love, the elect must be brought to God by heavy beatings, since they need to be chastised by the hands of the wicked to make them aware of their faults and to become receptive to grace.[32] In his 47th Sermon on the Book of Daniel, Calvin declares that evil comes to believers "that we may know that afflictions, miseries, and calamities, do not come apart from God's will, or without His Providence and determination . . . That we may say with Job: It is the Lord; with David: Lord, You have done it; with Hezekiah: To whom shall I complain, Lord, to You as my Judge? . . . Let us notice that it is God that hits us, and it is for our salvation. He wishes to mortify us from the world; He will not allow us to remain here overshadowed, but only to return us to Himself."[33] Calvin reassures his auditors that despite the confusions that reign here below, they can still confess that God rules all by His Providence and holds everything in His hand, and that at the parousia all mystery will be abolished. Meanwhile, they must believe that evil need not obscure Providence any more than snow can make the sun disappear.

Among Stauffer's conclusions on Calvin's sermons treating Providence are the following: contrary to the conclusions of many theologians, Calvin has no central, fundamental and controlling doctrine in his thought, but all that is Scriptural is essential; also that his teaching is invariable in 1200 Sermons and three editions of his *Institutes* prepared during the same period as his Sermons; but, at the same time, it is not totally homogeneous, because it is difficult if not impossible because of varying Biblical materials that cannot be wholly integrated. His final conclusion is that Calvin's preaching is characterized by "his strict Biblicism, and even, we are tempted to write, by his Biblical radicalism."[34]

3. Predestination As Providence

Calvin's further treatment of the doctrine of Providence, to which we now turn, is found in the third book of *The Institutes* in chapters xxi to xxiv. It is important to observe that Calvin treats the doctrine of Predestination formally as part of the doctrine of salvation, rather than under the heading of the doctrine of God. It is thus shown that predestination is part of the manner in which we receive the grace of Christ. Our method will be to follow Calvin in these chapters and later to add further insights on this highly controversial doctrine to be found in Calvin's other treatments of it in his sermons or in *A Treatise of the Eternal Predestination of God* which appeared in 1552, and was translated as *Calvin's Calvinism*, together with *Calvin's Defence of the Secret Providence of God.*
Election is important, according to Calvin, because it safeguards the fact that salvation is God's gift and not won by human beings. He says:

> We shall never be clearly persuaded, as we ought to be, that our salvation flows from the wellspring of God's free mercy until we come to know his eternal election, which illumines God's grace by this contrast; that He does not indiscriminately adopt all into the hope of salvation, but gives to some what He denies to others.[35]

Election also offers the practical advantage of safeguarding humility, as well as being the solid ground of confidence amid dangers, snares, and mortal struggles.[36]

Calvin warns, however, that the doctrine of predestination is to be sought in Scripture and not otherwise, for it is a hidden decree of God, and silence about it is to be avoided equally with a prying audacity and impudent attitude towards it.[37]

His famous definition goes as follows:

> We call predestination God's eternal decree, by which He determined with himself what he willed to become of each man. For all are not created in equal condition; rather, eternal life is foreordained for some, eternal damnation for others. Therefore, as any man has been created to one or the other of these ends, we speak of him as predestined to life or to death.[38]

Calvin adds to this definition later:

> As Scripture, then, clearly shows, we say that God once established by his eternal and unchangeable plan those whom He long before determined once for all to receive into salvation, and those whom on the other hand, He would devote to destruction. We assert, with respect to the elect, that this plan was founded upon his freely given mercy, without regard to human worth; but by his just and irreprehensible but incomprehensible judgment He has barred the door of life to those whom He has given over to damnation. Now among the elect we regard the call as a testimony of election. Then we hold justification another sign of its manifestation, until they come into the glory in which the fulfillment of that election lies.[39]

Hence, Calvin clearly teaches that there are three testimonies of election: Calling, Justification, and, beyond this life, Glorification.

Calvin then goes on to confirm the doctrine of Election from Scripture. He is most careful to insist that election is not because of any Divine foreknowledge of merit but due solely to God's sovereign purpose. Christ himself is "the clearest mirror of free election . . . and that He was not made Son of God by righteous living, but was freely given such honor so that He might afterward share his gift with others." Moreover, Ephesians 1:4a shows that Paul teaches we were chosen in Christ "before the foundation of the world."[40]

In addition, the election is to be holy, not because the recipients are already holy. The proof is that Jacob was elected and Esau was reprobated before they were born, as Paul makes clear in Romans 9:91-11.[41] For even greater proof, we have Christ's own witness about election in John's Gospel, in his saying: "All that the Father gives me will come to me" and "For this is the will of the Father . . . that whatever He has given me, I should lose nothing of it."[42] Calvin acknowledges that Ambrose, Origen, and Jerome held that God distributed his grace among men according as He foresaw that each would use it well, and that Augustine held the same view for a time, "but after he gained a better knowledge of Scripture, he not only retracted it as patently false, but strongly refuted it."[43] He then cites Augustine's saying for confirmation: "God's grace does not find, but makes those fit to be chosen."[44] Furthermore, Calvin repeats his warning about not prying into predestination, citing Paul's assertion in Romans 9:18: "God has mercy upon whomever He wills, and He hardens whomever He wills." By this, asserts Calvin, "men are warned to seek no cause outside His will."[45]

4. Calvin's Answers to Objections

The Reformer then deals with a series of objections against the negative aspect of Predestination, namely Reprobation. These objections he calls "false accusations". The first is: Does Election turn God into a tyrant? This is phrased by Calvin vividly thus: ". . . to devote to destruction whomever He pleases is more like the caprice of a tyrant than the lawful sentence of a judge". His blunt answer is: ". . . because He willed it. But if you proceed further to ask why He so willed, you are seeking something greater and higher than God's will, which cannot be found."[46] This seems a very unsatisfactory answer, but Calvin sheds further light in *Calvin's Calvinism*[47] where he says that he is rejecting the Schoolmen's consideration of the absolute or tyrannical will of God, wholly unacceptable to him because it distinguishes between the justice and the ruling power of God. He repeated the same objection in the famous *Congregation Faite en l'Eglise de Genève, en laquelle a esté traittée la Matière de l'Election Eternelle de Dieu.* There he simply refutes the objection by saying that Paul warns us against trying to be wiser than the Spirit of God.[48]

A second objection argues that the doctrine of Election takes away guilt and responsibility from men—the antinomian criticism. "Why should God impute those things to men as sin, the necessity of which He has imposed by his predestination?" Calvin certainly cannot be accused of stating the objections inaccurately or unfairly. He begins by asserting that God is the author of reprobation, while affirming that "the decree is dreadful I confess."[49] Calvin insists that God willed Adam's Fall and the consequent rejection of the reprobates with justice, and strongly denies any distinction between God's will and God's permission, because that makes God less than omnipotent.[50] Moreover, Calvin claims that it is perverse for the reprobate to ignore their own corrupt natures and to seek another source for their condemnation.[51]

A third objection is that the doctrine of Election leads to the criticism that God shows partiality towards persons. Calvin replies that election is not due to regard for a person, partiality in that sense, but solely to his great mercy. Scripture, Calvin contends, corroborates this assertion, for Acts 10:34 and Galatians 2:6 teach that the Lord has no favorites, while Galatians 3:38 demonstrates that God does not distinguish between Jew and Greek, while I Corinthians 1:26 recognizes that God did not originally call many who were of noble birth, or wise, or distinguished.[52]

A fourth objection contends that the doctrine of Election destroys all zeal for an upright life. The critic argues, says Calvin, "it makes no difference how he conducts himself, since God's predestination can neither be hindered nor advanced by his effort."[53] Calvin replies that the whole aim of election is holiness of life and so "it should goad us eagerly to set our mind upon it rather than to serve as a pretext for doing nothing." Also, it is an error to argue that a man trying to live an upright life will lose his labor, because the very endeavor of living in order to please God arises from election.[54]

The fifth and final objection is that Election makes all admonitions meaningless. Calvin counters with Ephesians 2:10 as rightly insisting that "we are God's work, created for good works, which He has prepared beforehand, that we should walk in them." He adds, "Let preaching take its course that it may lead men to faith, and hold them fast in perseverance with continuing profit."[55]

Calvin moves into the final chapter on Election by maintaining that Election is confirmed by the Calling of God. Faith, he insists is the work of Election, but that Election does not depend upon faith. In this two errors are to be avoided: "Some make man God's co-worker, to ratify election by his consent. Thus, according to them, man's will is superior to God's plan. Others . . . make election depend upon faith, as if it were doubtful and also ineffectual until confirmed by faith." [56]

Calvin strongly stresses the security of the perseverance of the elect under the protection of Christ. The linking of election to calling is a further source of assurance, but the chief security for the elect is that "Christ proclaims aloud that He has taken under His protection all whom the Father wishes to be saved." Here Calvin's New Testament authority is John's Gospel, chapter 6:37, 39 and chapter 17:6, 12. Yet he reminds his readers, again under Paul's guidance, not to be deluded by over assurance: "Let him who stands well, take heed lest he fall" (I Corinthians 10:12) and Romans 8:30, "Many are called, but few are chosen."[57] The conclusion must be that faith and calling are of little effect unless perseverance is added. But, the ground of security, Calvin again asserts, is that "there is no doubt when Christ prays for all the elect, He implores for them the same thing He did for Peter, that their faith may never fail." The clear conclusion is that whoever truly believes in Christ can never fall away.[58]

Calvin next exegetes Christ's statement "Many are called, but few are chosen" on the basis of two types of calling, the one general, the other special. The general calling is that God invites all equally to himself through the outward preaching of the Word; but the special calling is chiefly reserved for believers alone, for by the inward illumination of the Holy Spirit He causes the preached Word to dwell in their hearts. Yet sometimes, He also causes those whom He illuminates to partake of it only for a time. Then He justly forsakes them because of their ingratitude, and strikes them with greater blindness. [59]

Next, Calvin is concerned with God's dealings with the reprobate. If we ask what happens to them, Calvin replies: " . . . He sometimes deprives them of the capacity to hear his Word; at other times He rather blinds them by the preaching of it." Then Calvin makes the minatory statement that sermons are possibly effective to only 20% of a congregation: "If the same sermon is preached, say, to a hundred people, twenty receive it with the ready obedience of faith, while the rest hold it valueless, or hiss, or loathe it."[60]

The Reformer has still to deal with some apparent contradictions in Holy Writ: "God is said to have ordained from eternity those whom He wills to embrace in love, and those upon whom He wills to vent his wrath. Yet He announces salvation to all men indiscriminately." This seems to be contradictory, yet both statements can be made to agree, because God means that "his mercy is extended, provided they seek after it, and implore it. But only those whom He has illumined do this. And he illumines those whom He has predestined to salvation."[61] Finally, Calvin states: "Let this be our conclusion: to tremble with Paul at so deep a mystery; but if forward tongues clamor, not to be ashamed of this exclamation of his: 'Who are you, O man, to argue with God?' (Romans 9:20). For, as Augustine truly contends, they who measure Divine justice by the standard of human justice are acting perversely."[62]

It cannot be sufficiently emphasized that Calvin would not have presumed to commend double predestination unless he had believed that it upheld both the mercy and justice of God and that it was clearly expounded in the Word of God. The latter point is vigorously asserted in his *Treatise of the Eternal Predestination of God*, where he states: "I can declare with all truth that I should never have spoken on this subject unless the Word of God had led the way, as indeed all godly readers of my earlier writings, and especially of my *Institutes* will readily gather."[63] Further, although Calvin was awestruck by the decree of reprobation, he believed that it was affirmed by Christ's statement, recorded in Matthew 15:13 that every tree Christ's heavenly Father had not planted will be uprooted. On this Calvin commented that if his critics say "that this is no sign of reprobation, there is nothing so clear that it can be proved to them."[64] It should be noted that Edward A. Dowey, Jr. has warned that it is not enough to say that the doctrine of predestination exhibits Calvin's concern for the absolute sovereignty of God; rather, "for Calvin God is never merely sovereign. He is sovereignly good, sovereignly just, sovereignly merciful and gracious."[65]

One of the great mysteries, as Calvin willingly acknowledged, was that God foresaw the fall of Adam and the sins of all the generations of human beings that followed him. Hence, Calvin queried: "Whence does it happen that Adam's fall irremediably involved so many peoples, together with their infant offspring in eternal death, unless because it so pleased God . . . The decree is dreadful, I confess. Yet no one can deny that God foreknew what end man was to have before He created him, and consequently foreknew, because He so ordained by his decree."[66] Calvin, in defending this view, can only fall back on Augustine's argument that God's omnipotent goodness was able to bring goodness out of evil. But it is difficult to square God's justice with holding Adam's issue of many generations later guilty of the sin that was Adam's. No wonder that again and again Calvin returned to a declaration of faith beyond reason and a conviction of the transcendental wisdom and justice of God.

Calvin summed up his conviction on the doctrine of Election in his *Commentary on the Epistle to the Ephesians,* when expounding the fifth verse of the first chapter, namely, "He predestined us in love to be his sons through Jesus Christ, according to the purpose of his will." Calvin expresses this doctrine in terms of Aristotelian logic thus: "In this clause three causes of our salvation are expressed . . . The efficient cause is the good pleasure of God's will: the material cause is Christ: the final cause is the praise of his grace."[67] Later Calvin added a fourth cause: the formal cause is the preaching of the Gospel by which the goodness of God flows out to us.

While there are great difficulties in Calvin's doctrine of Reprobation, it does include some important stresses. Such is Calvin's insistence that we must not try to play God by distinguishing in the members of the Church those who are elect from those who are reprobate. This must be left to the Judge of the Great Assize at the end of history. The Reformer certainly recognizes that some show themselves to be reprobates as obstinate heretics while the conduct of others provokes scandal in the Church, and the Church must separate itself from both groups by excommunication; but, "even so, the disciplinary judgment of the church must in no way prejudge the definitive judgment of God."[68] As Wendel rightly comments: "Doubtless, the knowledge we have of reprobation is not merely theoretical and striking examples of it can convince us brutally of its reality; but we have no right to search out its effects in the life of the Church or in our relations with other men. We must not make ourselves the executors of judgments which we attribute with more or less resemblance of God. Predestination will only be fully revealed to us in the future."[69] But above all, the elect can rely for security on their growing and indissoluble union with Christ.[70]

5. Calvin's Dependence On and Independence of Augustine

Our next concern must be to try to assess the degree of Calvin's doctrinal dependence upon Augustine, as well as the difference between the two theologians.

On this we will benefit from the researches of Luchesius Smits, whose *Saint Augustin dans l'oeuvre de Jean Calvin*, translated from the original Dutch into French, is the definitive work on its theme. Clearly, Calvin is impressed by the fact that Augustine takes Scripture so seriously, but Smits says the great additional attraction was that Calvin was persuaded that "no one had understood as well the great scriptural mysteries of free will, of grace, or predestination, and of the sacraments. Nor had anyone synthesized the thought of antiquity so well as the African doctor."[71] He also emphasizes how frequently Calvin rejoices in the tribute of *totus noster est* or its equivalents.[72] Smits has statistics to substantiate Calvin's dependence upon Augustine either by direct citations or by clear references to him. Smits finds that Calvin's works reveal a total of 4,119 references to Augustine. It is equally interesting to discover that these are made up as follows: 1175 in the *Institutes*, 2214 in other theological treatises, 504 in the various commentaries on the Bible, 47 in the Letters, 33 in the Sermons, and 146 in the letters of authors cited by Augustine that Calvin used. The single work in which Calvin reveals his greatest indebtedness is Augustine's *Defensio servitutis arbitrii* which is referred to 431 times.[73] Second only to this, is Calvin's dependence upon Augustine's several Anti-Pelagian writings with a total of 649 references. It is notable that Calvin accepts in full Augustine's total denial of human free will and for the same reasons: to glorify the impact of God's transforming grace on humanity and to refuse to diminish any of the freedom and absolute control of the Divine will. Both theologians assert that man, apart from grace, is a veritable slave of evil, and that his only hope is to become a servant of Christ through the total obedience of faith.

Despite Calvin's considerable debt to Augustine, he is much more than a mere editor and repristinator of Augustine. There are decided differences of emphasis between the Catholic and the Protestant theologians. For Augustine the ultimate authority is the Catholic Church; for Calvin the final authority is Holy Scripture, because it is the Word of God to be Christologically interpreted and confirmed by the inner attestation of the Holy Spirit. Calvin's approach is expressed with admirable clarity in his Commentary on John, where he stated that the ultimate purpose of Scripture is to enable believers to find Christ there in both the Old and New Testaments, in the former in the Law and the Prophets as Messiah and Instructor, and in the latter as the Incarnate Word. He sums up: "The Scriptures are to be read with the purpose of finding Christ there." [74]

There is no question but that Calvin is far more determined to be the faithful expositor of Scripture than was Augustine. Consequently, the range, frequency, and length of his Biblical citations are greater than those of Augustine. Furthermore, Calvin has a decided preference for literal renderings of the Bible, rather than for risking subjective interpretations through allegorical hermeneutics, a practice which Augustine favored because it demanded greater meditation and resulted in greater ingenuity. Also, Calvin's mind is less addicted to speculation than Augustine's. Here one is inclined to concur with Edward A. Dowey, Jr. who repudiates the commonly expressed view that Calvin's teaching on reprobation is predominately a speculative and metaphysical motif, since it seems "unlikely that we have here a sudden abandonment of Calvin's whole method for a single experiment in philosophy, especially when he denied it so continuously." Rather, Dowey adds, "We have here one might say, a reckless consistency in working out of the Biblical teaching of the gratuitousness of divine mercy." [75]

It is surely the same rejection of a metaphysical distinction for fidelity to the Biblical witness that we find in Calvin's unwillingness to accept a distinction between God's actual willing and His Divine permission. Augustine was here probably attempting to defend God from active association with and determination of evil by thinking of Divine permission. This is totally rejected by Calvin, presumably because it diminishes God's omnipotence and denies God's wonderful ability to bring good out of evil. Calvin's refusal is expressed as follows:

> "But the word *harden*, when in Scripture it is attributed to God, doth not only signify (as certain tempering moderators would have it) a permission or suffering, but also the action of God's wrath." [76]

Theologically Calvin goes beyond Augustine in affirming (rather than inferring), not a single Predestination, but double Predestination. Augustine had a double predestination only by implication, and therefore his doctrine looked less harsh than Calvin's. Augustine emphasized the positive doctrine by which God had determined to save the elect by an act of gratuitous mercy, only abandoning the reprobate to the ruin which their sins have justly led them. Technically it is "preterition" rather than an act of damnation. It seems that Calvin was more open and forthright than Augustine in this respect: he was convinced that the negative action was God's, however incomprehensible and fearful to contemplate, because he firmly believed, as did Augustine, that men cannot accept or refuse the message of salvation if left to themselves, so the decision must therefore be God's alone, and it is better not to try to penetrate God's secret judgment in this decree. [77]

In conformity with his preference for a Scriptural basis for doctrine, and for a literal rather than a figural or allegorical and subjective interpretation, Calvin showed far less interest in speculative philosophy than Augustine did. This was because Calvin was convinced that philosophy was valueless in illuminating any mystery concerning the nature of God or His relations with human beings.[78] Calvin was, therefore, entirely disinterested in Augustine's speculations on the inner Being of the Trinity and of the supposed likeness to the Triune God in the triple functions of the human personality in, respectively, intellect, memory, and will.[79] Nor did Calvin in his theodicy make use of the Augustinian view that evil was merely negative, an absence of being, a *privatio* or *amissio boni.* [80]

Further, Calvin differed from Augustine in four aspects of his interpretation of predestination, the Fall, and original sin. First, in reference to the decree he is supralapsarian, that is, he holds that the decrees of election and reprobation are not due to the Fall but were made before it, and independently of it. Augustine, by contrast, is infralapsarian, arguing that we are condemned because we fell into sin with Adam's misuse of his free will. The second difference is that Augustine believes that fallen man still retains a spark of the Divine likeness, whereas Calvin believes then humanity since the Fall is totally corrupted. Third, Augustine maintains that Adam before the Fall was perfect, while Calvin asserts this was not so,[81] since Adam was not self-sufficient since he needed God and was blessed not because of his own good actions, but by participation in God. Fourth, while Augustine is aware of Adam's desire to be as God he places the major emphasis on the first man's concupiscence, whereas Calvin, also acknowledging the sexual appetite gives higher place to pride: "For not only did a lower appetite seduce him, but unspeakable impiety occupied the very citadel of his mind, and pride penetrated to the very depths of his heart." [82]

6. Negative Criticism

It remains only to evaluate Calvin's doctrine of Providence. At the outset it must be acknowledged that Calvin himself openly acknowledged the criticisms of his theodicy by his contemporaries, and, by implication, of future critics as well. Moreover, he expressed these objections with fairness, clarity and concision.

The major criticism of double predestination is the utter unfairness and injustice of God in damning the reprobate when, through their inheritance of corruption from Adam, they are incapable of obeying God unless He sends them his grace to give them faith and the empowerment of their wills to obey Him. In his Commentary on Paul's Epistle to the Romans, Calvin states the objection thus: "Because, therefore, it seemeth absurd that some should be preferred before others without desert, the forwardness of men maketh war with God, as though he gave unto the persons more than equity."[83] His critics could not have expressed the sense of Divine injustice more exactly.

This doctrine of double predestination can be accused of Divine favoritism to the elect and of injustice to the reprobate, as well as a denial of the freedom of the human will since the Fall of Adam. Those theologians such as St. Thomas Aquinas who argued that God chose the elect because He foresaw their positive response to his offer of salvation in Christ, have avoided these criticisms and left room for freedom in the acceptance of revelation. Furthermore, Calvin's response to this criticism is wholly unconvincing in asserting that God dooms the reprobate "to show forth the testimonies of his severity, that others might be terrified by so horrible examples, and also to set forth his power."83

Richard Stauffer tells us that in his sermons Calvin never says a word about free will.[84] This is incorrect, for in his sermons in his Commentary on the Book of Isaiah he definitely denies free will as a possible *preparatio evangelica*: "Note well, therefore, that all that belongs to our salvation proceeds from the grace of God, and that we must not imagine either free will or other preparations as the papists are even today still trapped in this belief, but we must acknowledge that there is nothing in us except malice and corruption until God shall have reformed us and we shall resemble Him . . ."[85]

This utter exclusion of free will in the response to God in salvation is usually defended by Calvin on the grounds that all goodness comes from God alone, that any granting of free will to humans only diminishes the sole freedom and absolute power of God, and thus men are ultimately total slaves to corruption apart from grace, has the ironic effect of causing men to blame God for human sin and to make virtue impossible. It is, of course, only in matters of faith that Calvin denies human freedom, for he acknowledges that there are secondary causes in all secular affairs.

In his lengthy study of the doctrine of predestination, J. B. Mozley concludes: "The predestinarian is at fault in assuming either the Divine Power, or original sin, as singly and of itself a legitimate basis of a system–in not allowing side by side with these premises a counter premise of free will and original power of choice."[86] Mozley adds that the predestinarian's mistake is that "He is unreasonably jealous for the Divine Attribute, and afraid that any original power assigned to man will endanger the Divine."[87] But the congruence of grace and free will must, therefore, remain a mystery.

The exclusion of all religious liberty from human beings in the matter of their salvation has laudable motives, including the desire to give all the glory to God and to keep human beings humble instead of boasting of their merits, and to safeguard the omnipotence of God and his total freedom, but these aims are achieved at the cost of leaving us with a deterministic Deity, who resembles Aristotle's unmoved Mover, rather than the God who patiently waits for the prodigal son to return and then runs to meet and embrace him. Daniel Migliore, writing of distorted images of Divine power, maintains that God imagined as a supreme monarch or Divine Dictator, "is a symbol of coercive power, the power of brute force and compulsion . . . sheer almightiness, unqualified omnipotence."[88] Migliore also maintains that the result of worshipping such an image of God is "fear, resentment, and rebellion."[89]

According to Jurgen Moltmann the God of Aristotle can only be characterized as a being who does not love in return those who adore Him for his perfections and beauty. Hence, He is immutable and impassible, and since He cannot suffer, one is tempted to add, insufferable! Moltmann calls him "a Narcissus with metaphysical powers, *Deus incurvatus in se.*"[90] The latter term, "God curved in on himself" is Augustine's term for man solely interested in himself because of his selfishness, and it seems a highly appropriate term for Aristotle's deity, complete in himself. C. S. Lewis vividly distinguishes between the God of Aristotle and the God of Christianity: "Hence I think that nothing marks off pagan theism from Christianity so sharply as Aristotle's doctrine that God moves the universe, Himself unmoving, as the Beloved moves a lover. But for Christendom 'Herein is love, not that we loved God but that He loved us.'" (I John 4:10).[91]

Augustine's and Calvin's deterministic Deity and their God of the eternal decree, which seems to prevent liberty in both God and humanity, has been the source of extreme criticism since the days of Arminius and John Wesley. Wesley's famous sermon on "Free Grace" based on Romans 8:32 listed eight different objections to predestination, the last being the fiercest criticism, namely, that it is blasphemous. "It is full of blasphemy; for it represents our blessed Lord as a hypocrite and dissembler, in saying one thing and meaning another–in pretending a love which He had not; it also represents the most Holy God as more false, more cruel, and more unjust than the devil; for in point of fact, it says that God has condemned millions of souls to everlasting fire for continuing in sin, for want of the grace He gives them not, they are unable to avoid."[92]

A closely allied criticism is expressed by Dakin in reference to the reprobate: "Calvin seems to lack deep feeling for human suffering, at least in his theological exposition. His doctrine is without pathos."[93] It has been already observed that even within the Church Calvin alleged that not more than 20 per cent would be among the elect,[94] and presumably those outside the Church in all centuries and among many, many nations, would reduce that percentage to a minimum. How could this be squared with Augustine's emphasis on the Divine *caritas*[95] or with Calvin's own glorying in the Divine mercy?[96]

One has no alternative but to conclude that Aristotelianism has muted the New Testament conception of God, and that the Christian doctrine of the Trinity should not let us forget that God the Father suffered in the death of his son, that his Son, the Christ, suffered and cried out in mental and physical agony on the Cross, and that the Holy Spirit groans with the entire suffering creation for the glorious liberty of the sons (and daughters) of God which is to be revealed. In the celebrated words of Dietrich Bonhoeffer, written in prison, "Only a suffering God can help."[97]

Finally, then, Calvin must be accused of attempting to square the universalist texts of Scripture with the Divine decree by misinterpreting them, as Augustine had done before him,[98] which had the unintended effect of reducing the Divine benevolence. Furthermore, even in analysing the conflicting views of the relationship of the Divine will to human wills, the domination of God overshadows the persistent patience and sacrificial love of God revealed in Christ.

7. Positive Criticism

What, then, can be said positively about Calvin's doctrine of Providence? Unquestionably there is much to admire in Calvin's devout reverence of God and his unfailing trust that the God of all the earth will prove to be just, however much the critics may "bark" (Calvin's word) to show their disagreement. For Calvin the controlling principle that gives its fullest meaning to life is that the supreme power in the universe is God and for all believers this is an immense consolation, especially in chaotic and critical times. Dakin reminds us that Calvin, by the doctrine of predestination, brings the soul into relationship with the one great abiding principle, the will of God, and that there was infinite comfort in that principle since God is "both the creator and sustainer of all things and at the same time the Savior and hope of the believer."[99]

Moreover, another advantage of Calvin's theology is that if one can be reasonably assured of being one of God's elect, this is an attitude that inspires unflinching courage. J. L. Motley, the historian, wrote that in his opinion, Calvinism's characteristic doctrine of double predestination made those who held it men of military valor: "The doctrine of predestination, the consciousness of being chosen soldiers of Christ, inspired those Puritans who founded the commonwealths of England, of Holland and of America, with a contempt of toil, danger, and death, which enabled them to accomplish things almost supernatural."[100] Calvin himself was undaunted, despite the difficulties and even dangers under which he worked as the Reformer of Geneva. Bearing Motley's tribute in mind, one also recalls the stirring words of advice Beza gave to the King of Navarre:

"Sire, it belongs to the Church of God, in whose name I speak, to endure blows rather than inflict them. But it will please your majesty to remember that she is an anvil that has worn out many hammers."[101]

The doctrine of election not only contributed courage, but also endurance, for Calvin taught Geneva and the Huguenots of France that Christ's elect were to expect suffering to test them, train their patience, and to keep them humble in their dependence upon God. Therefore, in a passage from a sermon on the Book of Isaiah, Chapter 13, Calvin reminded his auditory on February 22, 1557: "And it is an infinite consolation when we know that God, when punishing us yet does not cease to love us, and he hates those by whom we are persecuted. Therefore, when we are afflicted at God's hand He gives us this testimony that He has not at all forgotten us and that He punishes us only for a time that this may serve as medicine and make us contemplate His love."[102] This surely is Christian realism!

Furthermore, Calvin insisted that election kept Christ's true servants thoroughly humble in the obedience of faith. In this connection he wrote: "They who shut the gates that no one may dare seek a taste of this doctrine [election] wrong men no less than God. For neither will anything else suffice to make us humble as we ought to be, nor shall we otherwise feel how much we are obliged to God . . ."[103] In addition, Calvin assures those who are members of Christ's Body in faith that they have no need to be worried about their salvation: "The faithful should not doubt of their election, but they should consider that entirely resolved, since they are called to faith by the preaching of the Gospel, they are sharers of this grace of our Lord Jesus Christ and of the promise He has made them in his Name. For our Lord Jesus Christ is the foundation of these two things: to be precise, the promises of salvation and of our gratuitous election, which has been made since the creation of the world."[104] In his Commentary on Philippians, expounding chapter 4, verse 3, Calvin again felt it necessary to reassure his congregation thus: "In all those, therefore, in whom we see the marks of adoption shine forth, let us in the meantime reckon those to be the sons of God until the books are opened which will thoroughly bring all things to view." But with typical care

Calvin fences in the assurance immediately with a caution: "It belongs, it is true, to God alone now to know them that are His, and to separate the lambs from the kids; but it is our part to reckon in charity all to be lambs who in a spirit of obedience submit themselves to Christ as to their Shepherd and betake themselves to His fold, and remain there constantly. It is our part to set so high a value upon the gifts of the Holy Spirit, which He confers peculiarly on His elect, that they shall be to us the seals, as it were, of His election which is hid from us . . ."[105] To the very end Calvin's teaching always expresses the sublimity of reverence towards the living God, Judge and Savior, Creator, Sustainer and Controller of all things, animate and inanimate. Paul never had so faithful an interpreter as he! Furthermore, Calvin and Barth find the unity of theology in the following citation from the *Institutes* (III.xxiv.5):

> "Christ is the mirror wherein we must, and without self-deception may, contemplate our own election."

Notes

1 All citations from the *Institutes* in English will be from the Ford Battles translation in Vols. XX and XXI of *The Library of Christian Classics* (London: S.C.M. Press and Philadelphia: Westminster Press, 1961). This citation is from *Inst.* IV, viii, 5.

2 *Inst.* I, vii, 4.

3 *Commentary on Matthew*, XXVII, 9 (*Op.* 45, 749) and *Commentary on Hebrews* XI, 21 (*Op.* 55, 159). Both references are owed to Fran³ois Wendel, *Calvin: Sources et évolution de sa pensée religieuse* (2nd corrected edn., Paris: Labor et Fides, 1985), 118.

4 "John Calvin", p. 388 of ed. H. Cunliffe-Jones, *A History of Christian Doctrine* (Philadelphia: Fortress Press, 1980). See also Edward A. Dowey, Jr. *The Knowledge of God in Calvin's Theology* (New York: Columbia University Press, 1952), p. 218 f. Calvin experts disagree, however, as to whether he was an exponent of the verbal inspiration of the Scriptures or not. For an account of the different views, see "Was Calvin a Biblical Literalist?" by Richard C. Prust, *The Scottish Journal of Theology*, Vol. XX, (1967), pp. 312-328.

5 See P. Jacobs, *Prädestination und Verantwortlichkeit bei Calvin* (Neukirchen: Buchhandlung des Erziehungs verlein, 1937), pp. 64-71.

6 *Inst.* I, xvi, 1.

7 *Inst.* I, xvi, 4 and 5.

8 *Dieu, la création et la Providence dans la prédication de Calvin* (Berne: Peter Lang, 1978), p. 263.

9 *Ibid.*, cited by Stauffer in my translation.

10 *Inst.* I, xvi, 4.

11 *Calvin, Sources . . .* , p. 133.

12 *Inst.* I, xvi, 8.

13 *Inst.* I, xvii, 1.

14 *Ibid.*

15 *Ibid.*

16 Cited *Inst.* I, xii, 2.

17 *Ibid.*

18 *Ibid.*

19 A summary of *Inst.* I, xvii, 3-7.

20 *Inst.*, xvii, 7.

21 *Inst.* I, xvii, 8.

22 *Inst.* I, xvii, 9-11.

23 *Inst.* I, xvii, 12-14.

24 *Inst.* I, xvii, 12.

25 Cf. Augustine's *De ordine*, I.i-iii and *Enchiridion* xxiv, 95f.

26 *Inst.* I, xviii, 3.

27 *Inst.* I, xviii 4 and Augustine, *Letters*, 93.2; P. L. 33, 324.

28 From the 81st Sermon on II Samuel, cited Stauffer, *op. cit.*, p. 267.

29 48th Sermon on the Book of Job, cited Stauffer, *op. cit.*, p. 271.

30 *Op. cit.*, p. 273.

31 Sermon 93 on Deuteronomy, C. O., pp. 367-8.

32 Stauffer, *op. cit.*, pp. 278-9.

33 C. O. 42, p. 169.

34 *Op. cit.*, p. 304. The original reads: "La cinquième caracteristique de l'oeuvre homilétique consiste, dans son biblicisme strict, et même, serionsnous tenté d'écrire, dans son radicalisme biblique."

35 *Inst.* III, xxi, 1.

36 *Ibid.*

37 *Inst.* III, xxi, 2.

38 *Inst.* III, xxi, 5.

39 *Inst.* II, xxi, 7.

40 *Inst.* III, xxii, 1.

41 *Inst.* III, xxii, 5.

42 *Inst.* III, xxii, 7, citing John 6:37, 39.

43 *Inst.* III, xxii, 8. Augustine, *Retractations* I, xxiii, 2-4 (P. L. 32, 621).

44 Augustine's *Letters*, 186. 5. 15. (P. L. 33, 821). The original reads: "electio gratiae, non invenit eligendos, sed facit."

45 *Inst.* III, xxii, 11.

46 *Inst.* III, xxiii, 2.

47 *Calvin's Calvinism*, p. 266, originally printed in 1856 (republished by Eerdmans of Grand Rapids in 1950) is H. Cole's translation of two Calvin treatises, *A Treatise of the Eternal Predestination of God* and *Defence of the Secret Providence of God.*

48 *Op. cit.*, originally printed in 1562, reprinted in the *Corpus Reformatorum*, XXXI (Brunsvigae, 1870), p. 108b. Calvin cites Romans 9:20-21 to corroborate that his answer has Scriptural authority. (*Inst.* III, xxiii, 4).

49 *Inst.* III, xxiii, 7.

50 *Inst.* III, xxiii, 8.

51 *Inst.* III, xxiii, 9.

52 *Inst.* III, xxiii, 10.

53 *Inst.* III, xxiii, 12.

54 *Ibid.*

55 *Inst.* III, xxiv, 3.

56 *Ibid.*

57 *Inst.* III, xxiv, 6.

58 Luke 22:32 (*Inst.* III, xxiv, 6).

59 *Inst.* III, xxiv, 8.

60 *Inst.* III, xxiv, 12.

61 *Inst.* III, xxiv, 17.

62 *Ibid.*

63 *Corpus Reformatorum, Opera Calviniana*, vol. 8:265.

64 *Inst.* III, xxiii, 1.

65 *The Knowledge of God in Calvin's Theology*, p. 210.

66 *Inst.* III, xxiii, 7.

67 *Corpus Reformatorum*, vol. 51, p. 147. The original reads: *In hoc membro tres salutis nostrae causas exprimit . . . causa efficiens est beneplacitum voluntatis Dei: causa materialis est Christus: causa finalis, laus gratiae.*

68 *Inst.* IV, xii, 9.

69 *Calvin: Sources et Evolution de sa Pensée religieuse*, pp. 215-6.

70 *Inst.* III, xxi, 7.

71 Smits, *op. cit.*, I, p. 271. The book was translated into French by Egnbert Van Laethem and published at Assen in 1957.

72 *Ibid.* Examples given by Smits are: *Corpus Reformatorum* VI, 287; VI, 292; VI, 301; VI, 317; VI, 319; VI, 326; VI, 330; VI, 353; VI, 359; VIII, 266: *"totus noster est"* and IX, 149.

73 See the important table in Smits, *op. cit.*, p. 117 from which most of these statistics are derived.

74 Commentary on John 5:39; *Corpus Reformatorum*, vol. 48:125.

75 *The Knowledge of God in Calvin's Theology*, pp. 218-9.

76 *Commentary upon the Epistle to the Romans*, trans. C. Rosdell (Edinburgh: Calvin Translation Society, 1844), p. 265. Calvin is commenting on Romans 9:8.

77 *Inst.* III, xxiii, 1.

78 *Inst.* II, ii, 2.

79 *Inst.* I, xv, 4.

80 *Corpus Reformatorum*, vol. 8:353.

81 According to Calvin, Adam before the Fall was unstable and so subject to temptation as the 48th Sermon in *The Harmony of the Three Evangelists* indicates.

82 *Inst.* II, 1, 9.

83 *Commentary on the Epistle to the Romans* (Edinburgh, 1844: Calvin Translation Society), p. 270.

84 *Op. cit.*, p. 205.

85 *Sermons sur le livre d'Esaie* (Neukirchen: Kris Moers, 1961), p. 215.

86 *The Power of God* (Philadelphia: Westminster Press, 1983), p. 35.

87 *A Treatise on the Augustinian Doctrine of Predestination* (2nd edn. New York: Dutton, 1878), p. 307.

88 *Op. cit.*, p. 308.

89 *Op. cit.*, p. 41.

90 Moltmann, *Le Dieu Crucifié* (Paris, 1974; originally published in German in Munchen, 1972. The translation from the French is mine. The concept of the unsuffering God (*theos apathes*) comes from Aristotle's *Metaphysics*, XII, 1073 ff.

91 *The Problem of Pain* (New York: The Macmillan Company, 1959), p. 40.

92 Cited by Harry Buis, *Historic Protestantism and Predestinationism* (Philadelphia: Presbyterian and Reformed Publishing Co., n.d.), p. 94.

93 *Principles of Christian Theology* (1966), p. 224.

94 *The Mastery of Evil* (London: Centenary Press, 1941), p. 113.

95 A. Dakin, *Calvinism* (London: Duckworth, 1940), p. 26.

96 *Inst.* III, xxiii, 12.

97 Augustine gives no percentages, but admits that the elect are few (*pauci*) compared with the reprobates. *De Corrupt. et Gratia*, x. 28, and *De Civ. Dei*, XXI, 12.

98 Edward Dowey (*op. cit.*, p. 216) rightly insists that "The wrath of God is not such a basic characteristic of his relation to men as his mercy." Cf. Calvin's Commentary on Romans 1:18. Even so, the mercy of God is hardly enhanced by the doctrine of reprobation; and for the elect to delight in the justice of God in damning the reprobate argues more of pride than humility in them, and possibly even a smug sense of superiority.

99 *Letters and Papers from Prison* (revised and enlarged edition of 1971: 3rd edn. London: S.C.M. Press), p. 361.

100 *The History of the United Netherlands* (4 vols., 1861-68, New York: Harper & Brothers), IV, p. 548.

101 Cited A. M. Hunter, *The Teaching of Calvin*, p. 153, fn. 103.

102 *Sermons sur le Livre d'Esaie* (Neukirchen: Chr. Moers, 1961), *Supplementa Calviniana, Sermons inédits*, Vol. II, ed. Georges Barrois, p. 3.

103 *Inst.* III, xxi, 1.

104 *Congrégation Faite en l'Eglise de Genève, Corpus Reformatorum*, C. O. XXXVI, p. 114.

105 *Commentaries on the Epistles of Paul the Apostle to the Philippians, Colossians, and Thessalonians* trans. John Pringle (Edinburgh: The Calvin Translation Society, 1851), p. 287.

Chapter 5

Barth's Doctrine of Providence

Augustine, Aquinas, Calvin and Barth share remarkable similarities, but there are also basic differences. Two of them (possibly three) were twice-born theologians; that is, like Saul on the Damascus Road they were suddenly converted. Augustine, as his *Confessions* record,[1] hears the voice of a child calling, *Tolle et lege* ('Take up and read') and takes up Paul's Epistle to the Romans, opening it at Chapter 13, verse 13, where he reads the words that meet his dire need, "Not in rioting and drunkenness, not in chambering and wantonness, not in strife and envying; put ye on the Lord Christ, and make no provision for the flesh and its concupiscence."

Calvin, a quiet and profoundly modest man, typically buried in an unmarked grave, simply recorded the difference that grace had made *subita conversione* ('by a sudden conversion') with no further details. Karl Barth, the son of a professor of New Testament and Early Church History at Basle, would seem to have been a once-born Christian led from dawn to midday to the full light of grace, yet felt it necessary to reject almost all the nineteenth century theology he had been taught because it was relativistic and without any willingness to accept the irrational and evil elements in life as permanent. Hence he felt increasingly the need to formulate and to teach and preach a Christocentric and Trinitarian theology which was heralded in his great *Commentary* on Romans in 1919. This was surely a revolutionary, intellectual about-turn, if not a conversion. [2]

Aquinas, as far as we know, was a *once-born* genius, maturing without inner turmoil in the Christian faith and life, from his early days as a pupil in the leading Benedictine monastery of Italy, and living thereafter as a Dominican friar in Germany, France, and Italy, writing, preaching, arguing and contemplating, as a Christian philosopher, and celebrating the Eucharist with wonder and joy.

All four were outstanding preachers, and it is significant that Barth's reputation beyond Switzerland was made by his *Commentary* on the Epistle to the Romans of 1919, and that large sections of his *Die Kirchliche Dogmatik* are Biblical commentaries on specific texts. Moreover, during his years as a professor of theology at Basle he has preached on several successive Sundays to the inhabitants of the local jail, not forgetting his twelve years of pastoral ministry prior to his acceptance of a theological chair at Gottingen in 1921. As we have already seen, Augustine as Bishop of Hippo preached every Sunday as well as on most weekdays in his cathedral, and Aquinas was an outstanding preacher in the Order of Preachers. Again, Calvin's sermons and exegetical commentaries show how often he, too, proclaimed the Word of God from the pulpit.

The greatest difference between them all is Barth's denial and rejection of any value in natural theology, Calvin's recognition of a very limited value in natural theology, Augustine's conviction that philosophy can be a path towards the distinctively Christian revelation, and Aquinas's elevation of natural theology as a bridge leading to the supernatural theology or revelation; while all four agree that the knowledge of God in the Biblical revelation is absolutely primary, certain, and salvific.

It must also be noted that Calvin and Barth, even more than Augustine or Aquinas, were kerygmatic theologians, dominated by seeing the Bible as the normative custodian of Divine revelation, the chief written witness of God's communication to humanity. But for Barth, as some believe also for Calvin, while the Bible must play a dominant role in theology, it is not itself revelation, or "direct impartation" (in Barth's phrase). It is rather the mirror of God's Word for Calvin, while for Barth it is only the Holy Trinity - Father, Son, and Holy Spirit - who triply convey the Word of God, and if the Father is the initiator, the Incarnate Son of God is the revelation for our humanity, which is confirmed in faith by the Holy Spirit.

All four theologians were also men of remarkable courage, derived from faith. It seems as though Augustine's life was a perpetual battle between himself and heretics, whether these were Pelagians or, nearer home, the indefatigable and more numerous Donatists. And, as he aged, his task increasingly was to keep hope alive in the hearts of his hearers, who included many who were escapees from battered Rome to the North African coast, and the natives who were increasingly threatened by the barbarian invaders. The quiet scholar Calvin, who himself escaping from France to Basle by way of Geneva, was threatened by the reformer Farel with everlasting fire if he refused the call to assist him in establishing the Protestant faith and a truly Reformed Church in Geneva, that tempestuous city. His bravest act was to return to Geneva after three years of relief as pastor to the French Reformed Church in Strasbourg in which he had sought refuge on being expelled from Geneva for preventing scandalous and impenitent persons from receiving Holy Communion by fencing the Lord's Table. Aquinas, too, had to fight; not only Augustinian Catholics, but seculars and even bishops, and his name was mud for years in both Paris and Oxford.

Barth, too, had the courage of his convictions. It was his new theology which provided the thrust behind the "Confessing Church" in Germany which opposed Nazism and the Nazi-sponsored "German Church" movement. Barth's theology was the foundation of the famous Declaration of Barmen of 1934[3] and in the following year he refused to swear an oath of allegiance to Hitler and was dismissed from his theological chair at Bonn University.

Finally, all four are notable theologians of Grace, recognizing that this is entirely the undeserved gift of God to humanity, although the element of the wrath and judgment of God is far stronger in Augustine, Aquinas, and Calvin than it is in Barth, as seen in their doctrine of predestination. Grace is demonstrated as even mightier by Barth in his marvelously radical reinterpretation of predestination and reprobation, as will be seen later. It is significant that the distinguished Dutch theologian, B. C. Berkouwer, a convinced Calvinist, though differing from Barth, gave his study the generous title, *The Triumph of Grace in the Theology of Karl Barth.* Like Barth, Calvin has little interest in natural theology (that is the view that man by nature has the power to inform himself about God apart from revelation from God). Barth on this subject says: "In the face of the Cross of Christ it is monstrous to describe the uniqueness of God as an object of natural theology. In the face of the Cross of Christ we are bound to say that knowledge of the one and only God is gained only by the begetting of men anew by the Holy Spirit."[4]

Barth utterly rejects the *analogia entis* (the analogy of being, that is, any analogy suggesting that there is something in the being of man which has its analogue in the being of God), in favor of the *analogia fidei* (the analogy of faith, which is itself given by God). Augustine, and to a greater extent Aquinas, insist that the natural knowledge of God is real because man is made in the image of God, but recognize that it needs to be supplemented by special Divine revelation. Barth, in contrast, emphatically insists that it will be impossible to attain knowledge of God from the human side, and that true knowledge of God comes from "a reaching out, which has taken place and takes place from the side of God." (C.D. II, 1. p. 280). Augustine, however, is prepared to accept the traditional arguments for the existence of God, and Aquinas is happy in his *Summa* to explicate the *quinque viae*, or five arguments for God's existence, for he was firmly of the conviction that grace, far from contradicting nature, completes it. Augustine considers the witness of Plato and the Neo-Platonists as a valuable testimony to the existence of God, as Aquinas does Aristotle's philosophy. For Calvin, as for Barth, dogmatics—the exposition of Biblical theology systematically—is the best form of apologetics (defending the faith), or even of eristics (confuting the opposition), by showing the depth and relevance of the Christian revelation.

The differences among these four theologians are also considerable. The differences are partly those of their historical contexts. Augustine lived in the Dark Ages of the fourth and fifth centuries, the years of the break-up of classical culture and the time of the onslaught of the barbarians on the Roman Empire. He began as a rhetorician, then became an amateur philosopher, and finally developed into a theologian of great originality, combining all three disciplines. His heart and mind are bared in *The Confessions* so that we know him better than any man before him, so honest and radical in his analysis. Augustine was also a great defender of the faith against heretics. Aquinas, too, had his philosophical and theological enemies to fight, but he was occasionally treated as a heretic himself! He had to counter the largely anti-theological impact of the newly-discovered treatises of Aristotle, especially those translated by and commented on by the Arab philosophers, Avicenna and Averroes. He also had to contend with Franciscan Platonists, like John Peckham (later to be Archbishop of Canterbury) who attacked his work in 1270, and his reputation with the even more serious condemnation of the 219 Aristotelian and Averroist articles by the Bishop of Paris, Etienne Tempier, in which twenty Thomist articles were included in 1277, three years after St. Thomas's death. Despite the opposition he managed to Christianize Aristotle, and he has become the most honored Catholic theologian in history, and the glory of the Order of Preachers.

Our two remaining theologians are Protestants. Calvin was a dedicated humanist scholar living in the Renaissance Europe of the sixteenth century, when the ominous split between Catholicism and Protestantism took place, and he was the outstanding Biblical theologian of the Reformation and its ablest church administrator. Barth is a man of this century, acutely aware of all the attacks on Christianity since the Enlightenment, and the defender (as well as critic) of the Church, who appears to be a traditionalist, but is in fact *Neo*-orthodox, and who changed the title of his *magnum opus* from *Christian Dogmatics* to *Church Dogmatics* because it is a theology for the Body of Christ and therefore must be centered on Christ, not on culture. It is also the expression of a man of great culture and historical learning,[5] with a marvelous sense of humor, and great brilliance, who–in the deepest sense–is marked by the obedience of faith in the Incarnate Christ.

1. Barth's Doctrine of Scripture

At the outset of our study of Barth it is important to understand Barth's doctrine of Scripture. He insists, in the first place, that we as humans do not decide that the Bible is the Word of God.

Simply as humans, we may find mistakes in it or dislike one or another of the characters who speak of God in the Bible. But the Bible proves to be the Word of God, because God overmasters us through its proclamation, creating faith in us. "Belief that the Bible is the Word of God presupposes, therefore, that this overmastering has already taken place, that the Bible has already proved itself to be the Word of God, so that we can and must recognize it to be such."[6]

In the second place, the Bible itself is not the Divine revelation: "It witnesses to God's revelation, but that does not mean that God's revelation is now before us in any kind of divine revealedness. The Bible is not a book of oracles; it is not an instrument of direct impartation. It is genuine witness."[7]

Thirdly, the only possible attitude for receiving the Bible as the Word of God is prayerful and humble obedience, hoping that the miracle of faith will come through it to us from God. Barth writes: "There is only one Word of God as that is the Eternal Word of the Father which for our reconciliation became flesh like us and has now returned to the Father, to be present to His Church by the Holy Spirit. In Holy Scripture, too, in the human word of his witnesses it is a matter of his Word and its Presence." Moreover, one cannot even say that the Bible has the attribute of being or even the potency of being the Word of God, for that would violate God's freedom and sovereignty to speak to a person through that Word, for God "is Lord over the Bible and in the Bible."[8] We cannot say that the Word of God is tied to the Bible; on the contrary, we have to say "that the Bible is tied to the Word of God"[9] and we recognize that it is by a free decision of God that we believe or fail to believe.

Christ, according to Barth, is concealed from us in His eternal presence as the Word of God in heaven while we are now living on earth and in time. "He is revealed only in the sign of His humanity, and especially in the witness of His prophets and apostles. But by nature these signs are not heavenly-human, but earthly–and temporal-human. Therefore the act of their institution as signs requires repetition and confirmation. Their being as the Word of God requires promise and faith–just because they are signs of the eternal presence of Christ."[10] And these can only come from the work of the Holy Spirit in the Church.

Barth adds that the Church must pray for the Bible in reading and preaching to be the Word of God here and now, and that the Holy Spirit may freely apply the grace of God to the assembled congregation. The fulfillment of that prayer "that the Bible is the Word of God here and now in virtue of the eternal, hidden, heavenly presence of Christ–that is the divine side of the life of the Church. Its reality cannot be doubted: the fullness of the reality of the Church with the Bible lies in this divine aspect."[11]

Barth concludes an eighty-page exposition of the authority of Holy Scripture in this fashion: "Scripture is recognized as the Word of God by the fact that it is the Word of God. This is what we are told by the doctrine of the Holy Spirit . . . And by the Holy Spirit the witnesses of His (Christ's) humanity became and are also witnesses of His eternal Godhead, His revelation was apprehended by them, and through them it is apprehended by us. When we say, 'Through the Holy Spirit' we mean by God in the free and gracious act of His turning to us. When we say 'By the Holy Spirit' we say that in the doctrine of Holy Scripture we are content to give the glory to God and not to ourselves." [12]

According to Barth, the Word of God is primarily the speech of God the Father to the eternal Son, and secondarily, God's gracious Word to humanity through Christ, most fully manifested in Christ's Incarnation, and now revealed by the Holy Spirit in faith in the witness of the heavenly Christ through the writings of the prophets and apostles. For contemporary humans it takes three forms: revealed, written, and proclaimed.[13] Finally, for Barth the Word of God is the living Word of Christ. He stressed this in the famous opening Article of the Declaration of the Synod of Barmen: "Jesus Christ, as He is attested to us in Holy Scripture, is the one Word of God which we have to hear and which we have to trust and obey in life and in death." And, as Herbert Hartwell points out, Barth in his *Church Dogmatics* gives it a special commentary at the end of his section on the Knowability of God, but also uses it as his thesis for the section on 'The Glory of the Mediator' which begins his teaching on Jesus Christ as the true Witness.[14] One cannot insist too strongly that Barth's Biblical theology is Trinitarian and Christocentric continually and consistently, and Barth would urge that this is the only authority it has or that any church theology, preaching or celebration of the Sacraments has. One is bound also to agree with Hartwell's judgment that Barth's *Church Dogmatics* is filled with often extensive exegetical discourses thus offering "a whole series of commentaries" and that "this Dogmatics is a very mine of sermon material." [15]

2. Providence Manifested in Election

In dealing with the doctrine of providence, Barth will not begin, as previous theologians have done, with a general idea of God, and speak of such attributes as His Omniscience, Omnipotence, and Justice. Rather, as he began his *Dogmatics* with the doctrine of the Word of God and followed it with an initial and specific exposition of the Doctrine of the Trinity of God as Father, Son, and Holy Spirit, so he will begin with the Doctrine of Election. For Barth the wonder and glory of the Christian faith is found in the infinite condescension and the self-emptying of God in the Incarnation of Jesus Christ, very God and very man. So, after a reasonably short account of the perfections of God as love and freedom,[16] Barth in a radically revised doctrine of Election enables us to see the divine providence most strikingly as a preparation for human salvation in Christ. Thus, in following Barth's own procedure, we shall treat first of the Election of God and, only secondly, of God's triple work in providence as preserving, accompanying and ruling the world for the benefit of the humanity He loves.

As the editors of the English translation of volume III, part 2 of the *Dogmatics* explain Barth's approach: "Like creation, providence is thus to be understood on the presupposition of the election of grace fulfilled in Jesus Christ and the covenant of grace concretely actualized in salvation history."[17] Thus providence in Barth's view must be seen as the fidelity of God the Lord of history to the creatures He has made and to whom He has joined Himself in Jesus Christ as Emmanuel, God with us. Thus for Barth "the doctrine of election is the sum of the Gospel because of all words that can be said or heard it is the best: that God elects man; that God is for man too the One who loves in freedom. It is grounded in Jesus Christ because He is both the electing God and elected man in One . . . " The function of this doctrine, Barth continues, "is to bear basic testimony to eternal, free and unchanging grace as the beginning of all the ways and words of God." [18]

Barth finds the Augustinian and Calvinian doctrine of predestination unacceptable for a variety of reasons. He insists that God's "first and last word is Yes and not No."[19] He finds the traditional doctrine a confusion of Yes and No, as well as an ambiguity that weakens the Gospel. He refers to Max Weber's criticism of its "pathetic inhumanity" as one great shadow and cites Weber's account of Milton's response to the Calvinian interpretation of the doctrine as follows: "Though I may be sent to Hell for it, such a God will never command my allegiance."[20] Barth believes that Calvin buttressed his doctrine by his hard experience of the many impenitent and impudent hissers at the preaching of the Gospel in church which he thought comprised 80% of the congregation.[21] Barth tends to agree with Heinz Otten that it was for the purposes of edification that Calvin in this matter relied partly on experience and partly on Scripture.[22]

Barth finds four unsatisfactory sources for the development of the traditional doctrine of predestination: first, an existing system not founded on grace; second, the practical utility of the doctrine as minatory but which is no guarantee of truth; thirdly, experience which begins with man not God; and, finally, a doctrine of divine sovereignty which begins with an abstract deity and not the electing god of Scripture.[23] Scripture, Barth maintains, directs us to Israel as the partner of God's covenant and finally to the ultimate man of Israel, Jesus Christ the Messiah. Jesus is the foundation of the doctrine in a double sense as both electing God and elected.[24]

In his positive exposition Barth asserts: "In its simplest and most comprehensive form the dogma of predestination consists, then, in the assertion that the divine predestination is the election of Jesus Christ." But this can be "divided into the two assertions that Jesus Christ is the electing God and that He is also elected man."[25] Thus the Son is elected by God the Father, and yet He is also the Subject of election as God, and as man He is the passive object of election. The importance of this passive election of Jesus is that it enables us to see what predestination always is, namely, the acceptance of man by God's free grace, for even as man there is no merit in Jesus for He is conceived by the Holy Spirit and thus by grace alone. The fact that God the Son participates in this election means that we need no longer speculate about the hidden meaning of the *decretum absolutum*[26] and God's intentions therein, for now they are known through Christ's Incarnation as full of grace. They are no longer shadows but light from the Light of the world. The decree is no longer inscrutable but the revelation of Divine mercy and utterly undeserved grace.

Next Barth turns to the three implications of this election as he envisages them. We see, first, that God is gracious in all His ways and works with humanity. Next, since Christ is elected to vicarious obedience and suffering and is paradoxically elected to rejection as the slain Lamb of sacrifice, we recognize anew the sheer undeserved grace of our election and its infinite generosity as a gift from Christ. Thirdly, seeing the faithfulness of Jesus to the Father and of the Father to the Son, election is perceived as enabling us to love and honor in Jesus the priest and victim as well as the divine justification and its representative.[27]

Barth then goes on to review the Supralapsarian and Infralapsarian viewpoints with reference to the decree of predestination, finally coming down on the side of supralapsarianism. Barth thinks it likelier as well as more hopeful that God in eternity was thinking of man as potentially created and potentially fallen, rather than of man already viewed as created and fallen. He approves of Supralapsarianism, when purified, as attempting to say "that in the beginning of all things in the eternal purpose of God before the world and before history, there was the electing God and elected man, the merciful and just God, and over against that God from all eternity *homo labilis*, man sinful and lost."[28]

Barth then goes on to expound the christological approach to predestination as an alternative to the absolute decree of Augustine and Calvin. He argues that the election of Christ demands faith and confidence in God which is obedience to God. Barth's own radical revision of the doctrine appears in the following statement: "We cannot believe in the *decretum absolutum*. We can only look at it and then forget it, turning elsewhere for the arbitrary satisfaction of religious needs. We cannot place any confidence at all in the *decretum absolutum* and obedience to it is quite inconceivable. The substitution of the election of Jesus Christ for the *decretum absolutum* is, then, the decisive point in the amendment of the doctrine of predestination." [29]

The striking originality in Barth's reinterpretation of predestination is seen in his maintenance that there is only one reprobate and rejected–and that is Jesus Christ. "Man is not rejected. In God's eternal purpose it is God Himself who is rejected in His Son. The self-giving of God consists . . . in the fact that He is rejected in order that we might not be rejected. Predestination means that from all eternity God has determined upon man's acquittal at His own cost. It means that God has ordained that in the place of the one acquitted He himself should be perishing and abandoned and rejected–the Lamb slain from the foundation of the world." [30]

One other criticism Barth had of the traditional doctrine of predestination was that it was excessively individualistic. This he attempted to remedy in his own reconstruction by insisting that primarily the election of God is the election of the community, of Israel as the divine judgment, and of the Church as the divine mercy. "The election of grace, as the election of Jesus Christ, is simultaneously the eternal elections of the one community of God by the existence of which Jesus Christ is to be attested to the whole world summoned to faith in Jesus Christ. This one community of God in its form as Israel has to serve as the representation of the divine judgment, in its form as the Church the representation of divine mercy. In its form as Israel it is determined for hearing, and in its form as the Church for believing the promise sent forth to man. To the one elected community of God is given in the one case its passing, and in the other its coming form."[31] These two forms of the community correspond to the double predestination of Jesus Christ, for He is both the crucified Messiah of Israel and the risen Lord of the Church.[32] Israel's service is to reflect the deserved judgment from which God delivers man, while the Church serves by reflecting the undeserved mercy of God.[33] Barth is careful to stress the unity between the communities also, by reminding the Church that it has a pre-existent life in Israel and the elect in Israel, climaxing in Jesus as the elect One. Barth also emphasizes the mercy of God, and the existence of Jewish Christians which keeps Gentiles remembering that they are rescued from the same judgment and saved by the same mercy.[34]

Barth next follows with an extensive treatment of the election by God of the individual. This election is particularly concerned with the autonomous individuality of the sinners who desire to be a law unto themselves, and thus set themselves against God. To such the election offers forgiveness and a true individuality.[35]

An important concern of Barth's is to distinguish between the elect and the rejected. The former are elect because of a distinction in God's relation to them and part of the community so elected to which they have assented. They *recollect* that they would be rejected apart from their election in Christ, and they *expect* for the others that they will ultimately not be rejected, because they cannot negate their election in Jesus Christ, however much their conduct would indicate the opposite.[36]

Inevitably, one is bound to wonder whether Barth is proposing universalism in affirming that the rejected cannot overwhelm their election in Christ? But in fact Barth rejects this as "historical metaphysics" since only Christ knows whether all will finally he brought into the kingdom of God. Barth does not reject the possibility of the final inclusiveness, but he dare not affirm it for that would be to foreclose the freedom of the sovereign Lord and God. "Just as the gracious God does not need to elect or call any single man, so He does not need to elect or call all mankind. His election and calling do not give rise to any historical metaphysics, but only to the necessity of attesting to them on the ground that they have taken place in Jesus Christ and His community."[37]

The elect are differentiated from others through their calling. "But their calling–the work of the Holy Spirit–is that by means of the community the election of Jesus Christ may be proclaimed to them as their own election, and that they may be assured of their election by faith in Jesus Christ by whom it was brought about."[38] The task and privilege of each of the elect is to be a messenger of God, an apostle: "This is his service and commission. It is for this purpose that he may represent and portray the glory of the grace of God. It is in this that he may be grateful and blessed. He is sent. He is an apostle. The reason for this is the election of Jesus Christ to be an apostle of grace. Its context is the apostolate of grace which is the meaning and order of the life of His whole community. The determination of the elect is to allow the light which has kindled within himself to shine . . . "[39]

How, we may ask, are the rejected to be determined? Barth defines a rejected man in the following manner: "A 'rejected' man is one who isolates himself from God by resisting his election as it has taken place in Jesus Christ. God is for him; but he is against God. God is gracious to him; but he is ungrateful to God. God receives him; but he withdraws himself from God. God forgives him his sins; but he repeats them as though they were not forgiven. God releases him from the guilt and punishment of his defection; but he goes on living as Satan's prisoner. God determines him for blessedness, and His service; but he chooses the joylessness of an existence that accords with his own pride and aims at his own honor. The rejected man does exist in his own way alongside the elect. We do not fully understand the answer to the question concerning the determination of the elect if we refuse to consider the situation of the others, the rejected."[40]

Next Barth indicates that the rejected have three functions to fulfill: to represent the man who needs the Gospel; to manifest what is negated and what is overcome in the Gospel; and, finally, to give a futureless man a future in the Gospel, that is, to hear and believe.[41] All this is based on a subtle analysis of the act, attitude and end of Judas Iscariot.[42]

Is there, then, hope for all of the rejected? In what Geoffrey Bromiley calls Barth's "incipient universalism"[43] there is such hope. Barth concludes his final paragraph on the doctrine of election with the following statement: "The rejected as such has no independent existence in the presence of God. He is not determined by God merely to be rejected. He is determined to hear and say that he is a rejected man elected."[44]

3. Criticisms of Barth's Doctrine of Election

Before proceeding to the more traditional approach to providence expounded by Barth in the *Church Dogmatics*, III, 3, the critiques that have been made of Barth's doctrine of election must first be considered.

Emil Brunner does not refer directly to Barth's doctrine of election, but in his criticisms it is clear that he has Barth in mind, for he criticizes what is original in Barth and appears in no other theologian, namely the concept that Christ is both Subject and Object of election. While he would appear to agree with Barth that the doctrine should be based on Biblical and not on speculative foundations, his major objection rests on his view that Barth is not Biblical enough. His chief criticism is that Barth fails to recognize the dialectical conjunction of holiness and love in God, for, in Brunner's view, the Bible asserts that the holy and merciful God, who has chosen all who believe in Him from all eternity, also rejects those who refuse the obedience of faith.[45] As a consequence, he has to reject Barth's teaching that Jesus is the only elect and only reprobate for this means that believers and unbelievers never come under the wrath of the holy God and thus, avers Brunner, Barth contracts the New Testament's insistence upon a final judgment at the end of history at the Great Assize. Furthermore, Brunner rejects Barth's assertion that Jesus is both the Subject of election and the only reprobate on another ground. This is the serious critique that Barth makes the God-man eternally pre-existent and thus undervalues the historicity of Christ's Incarnation.[46] In addition, Brunner claims that "The error in the doctrine of universal salvation is not that it leaves the door of divine possibility *open*, but that it leaves *this door only* open, and closes the door on the other possibility."[47] But Brunner, too, forgets if a door is left open, it is also possible that God in His sovereign will may close it. It is interesting that the serious charge of an inadequate understanding of the relationship of the divine and human natures in Christ, but in another form, is made by

Herbert Hartwell, who declares that the assertion that the Son of God is the Subject of the person of Jesus Christ casts a doubt on the true humanity of Jesus Christ in asserting the exclusively divine nature of the Subject of the being of Jesus Christ for that leaves Christ with an abstract human nature. He adds that "it is not impossible to think of the subject of the person of Jesus Christ as being from the beginning both divine and human without falling either into the Nestorian heresy of dividing Jesus Christ into two persons or into the heresy of Adoptionism, with the Spirit of God blending at the Incarnation and in a manner we cannot comprehend with the human center of consciousness, the human ego."[48]

Another critic, Henry Buis, offers two main objections to Barth's doctrine of election. Barth, he says rightly, wishes to leave the number of the elect indeterminate, but did not make this equal to the number of human beings. This looks like *apokatastasis* (universal restoration), but Barth will neither affirm it or deny it. This ambiguity is caused by the fact that Barth insists on both the refusal to limit God's freedom, and also because he cannot believe that the wickedness of humanity is superior to grace. Buis's second objection is that in Barth's affirmation that the basic difference between believers and unbelievers is simply that the unbeliever does not know as yet that he is elected, leads to such "an emphasis on the sovereignty of grace that he seems to empty human decision of any meaning whatsoever."[49]

A more sympathetic critic and one who has been the chief translator of Barth's *Die Kirchliche Dogmatik* into English is Geoffrey W. Bromiley, who praises the Christological and ecclesiological foci in Barth's doctrine. He also approves Barth's refusal of a balanced double predestination,[50] but he adds that while Barth rejects the abstract necessity of universalism as the logical consequence of the election of all in Christ, "it is not apparent why, in his view, the Holy Spirit in His ministry of calling should not positively fulfill in all individuals the one eternal will of the triune God."[51] Bromiley concludes: "The ambivalence at this decisive point–will all be saved or not, and if not, why not?–by no means outweighs the solid merits of Barth's presentation. Nevertheless, it undoubtedly casts something of a shadow over them, particularly in view of what seems to be the solid and consistent witness of scripture to eternal perdition as well as eternal salvation."[52]

Two of the most stringent critics have been theologians of the Reformed Church, Fred H. Klooster, an American, and the distinguished Dutch theologian, G. O. Berkouwer. Klooster will be treated briefly and Berkouwer at greater length. Klooster points out that for Barth election and reprobation are not equally rooted in the will of God since God wills election, but He does not will reprobation, adding "There are, in fact, these two classes of men, the called and the uncalled, the believing and the godless, and therefore the elect and the *apparently* rejected, the Community of God and the world." In citing Barth at II, 2, p. 351, he has, however, italicized the word "apparently". Klooster then goes on to say that Barth accuses Calvin in double predestination of speaking of an unknown God, but the charge can be returned to Barth who leaves open what the freedom of God might do for the supposedly elect or the supposedly reprobate. Consequently, "The frontier from election to rejection and vice versa can be repeatedly crossed and criss-crossed."[53] This criticism does not do justice to the dominance of election in Barth, but it does leave uncertainty for the rejected, it is true. More to the point, however, is Klooster's criticism that with the objective universal election in Christ Barth "minimizes the Scriptural warning against apostasy, as well as the call to repentance and faith. The total impact of Barth's theology tones down the desperateness of the sinner's situation as described in Scripture."[54] Finally, says Klooster, the effect of Barth's doctrine is that "Hence the urgency of preaching is gone, and the biblical significance of the call to repentance and faith loses its relevance."[55] Unquestionably Barth's warning to the Church not to take unbelief too seriously could have this result. Others, however, have said with equal intensity that there is a greater desire to preach the Gospel as good news because of Barth's redefinition of the doctrine of election. [56]

The most careful and detailed critic of Barth's *Dogmatics* is G. C. Berkouwer in his book, *The Triumph of Grace in the Theology of Karl Barth.* He counters what he considers to be a slander of Barth's, namely that the Swiss theologian asserts that Calvin, for all his emphasis on election, did not see that Christ was more than the elect means in the hands of the electing God the Father, but must be seen as Himself the electing God.[57] Berkouwer flatly denies this and makes his point by citing the following sentence of Calvin's: "But if we have been chosen in Him [Christ] we shall not find assurance of our election in ourselves; and not even in God the Father, if we conceive Him as severed from His Son."[58]

Berkouwer's serious conflict with Barth is concentrated in Barth's paradoxical statement that, as a result of the objective or ontological election of all in Christ, the consequence is "the impossible possibility of sin."[59] Berkouwer objects not only to the inconsistency in Barth, but also to the latter's lack of seriousness about the continuing reality of sin and also the danger of sin in human life. Further, he claims that Barth's argument that a mere knowledge of Christ's objective election of all is inadequate enough, since salvation subjectively requires repentance and faith and a vigorous proclamation of the wrath of God against sin. In addition, Berkouwer insists that Barth in his Christology has exceeded the boundaries of accepting the essential mystery of the union of the divine and human natures in the Incarnate Christ. Finally, Berkouwer takes radical exception to what he considers a seriously defective eschatology in Barth, due to its negativity. Each of these charges warrants a fuller explication.

Berkouwer believes that these weaknesses spring from inadequate attention to the fullness of the Scriptural witness, and particularly because " . . . Barth's Jesuscentric thinking is the decisive factor in his theology."[60]

First, we must examine the charge of the absence of a satisfactory correlation of Barth's near universalism of salvation with an adequate subjective transformation as its consequence. It must now be noted, says Berkouwer, that although Barth, on the one hand, speaks anthropologically about the ontological impossibility of sin, he speaks, on the other hand, of man's "ability" to sin, even though this is an "insane" ability. This cannot but give rise to questions, since Barth rejects in countless variations the idea of the "possibility" of sin. On this point Berkouwer concludes:

"If sin is ontologically impossible a transition from wrath to grace in the historical sphere is no longer thinkable." [61]

As to the failure to be serious about man's sinful condition, although the New Testament requires humans to struggle against its power, Berkouwer thinks Brunner's critical analogy admirably fits Barth's too easy account of salvation and his unwillingness to recognize the continuing danger of sin. Brunner suggested that this view of the human predicament is as if men were threatened with shipwreck at sea, but "In reality, however, they are not all on a sea in which they can founder, but in shallow water in which they cannot drown. They just do not know it."[62]

Barth, says Berkouwer, does not think that our liberation from the threat of sin and the danger of chaos is a matter of the future, since it has been finally overcome in Jesus as Victor over it on the Cross, so that for Barth chaos is only dangerous in appearance. It is only our blinded eyes that see it as dangerous menace. However, Berkouwer asks whether this is how Scripture sees this triumph. He answers his own questions thus: "On the one hand, we constantly meet in the Bible the appeal not to fear, to be of good courage and to believe steadfastly in the victory of Jesus Christ. On the other hand, we see that the believer is continually called to resistance and struggle."[63] To substantiate this claim Berkouwer cites Hebrews 12:4: "In your struggle against sin you have not yet resisted to the point of blood" and Hebrews 4:2: "The good news came to us as to them; but the message did not benefit them, *because it did not meet with faith in the hearers*." (Berkouwer's italics) Berkouwer's apt comment is: "These words just do not leave room for the view that the human decision has been already been taken, is given and is involved in the encounter with revelation." [64]

A third serious criticism of Berkouwer's involves Barth's interpretation of the Incarnation. Berkouwer states that Barth sees in the Crucifixion that God Himself "is the true God in the suffering and obedience of Christ" and "the triumph of grace manifests itself in the revelation of *this* suffering and of *this* obedience of God."[65] This is, says Berkouwer, "theopaschitism of a new form."[66] Barth is unwilling to have a general conception of deity and then to consider Christ as partaking of this deity; rather he wishes Christ not be the point of departure to know who God is. The result is that the deity is to be understood as humiliation and not as sovereign will or glory—for the glory is in the humiliation for Barth. But Berkouwer insists: "It will not do to say that in powerlessness and in death the omnipotence and the life of God are revealed."[67] Barth is inconsistent here, says Berkouwer, for again and again Barth says that God's omnipotence is revealed in the fact that Jesus Christ is Lord over life and death. Also Barth speaks of "God Himself" as suffering and obedient—not just in Christ's human nature—but in Himself as *vere Deus*, which inevitably leads to the conclusion of "a tension and an obedience in God Himself, to an 'above' and a 'below' in Him," and this "can only be characterized as speculation."[68] The relation of the divine and human in the Incarnate Christ is, says Berkouwer, "an incomprehensible mystery" and should force us to recognize the limitations placed on our thinking.[69]

Berkouwer further argues that the New Testament insists on the significant transition from the humiliation of the Incarnation to the exaltation at the Resurrection and Ascension, but Barth sees the exaltation and glorification in the Incarnation itself. Thus, says Berkouwer, Barth unwarrantably denies the temporal element dividing the two estates and wrongly telescopes them.[70]

4. Barth's General Doctrine of Providence

It is necessary next to consider Barth's general Christian doctrine of providence and to summarize the 531 pages of the English translation of volume III, part 3 of Barth's *Christian Dogmatics* with the utmost brevity.

Providence is different from predestination, already considered, but it is concerned with the execution of that decree. Providence can be interpreted as an act of faith in God's Word which reveals Him as sovereign and loving Lord of the creature, through faith in Christ. Furthermore, God is known in revelation, not primarily from history since world history is a riddle unless it is interpreted by the revelation of salvation history, in which God is recognized in the covenant of grace.[71]

God's providence is seen in terms of the standard triple aspects of God's care for His creature, man, as *conservatio*, *concurrus*, and *gubernatio*, which Barth defines Christologically as preserving the creature for His covenant purpose and because of the advocacy of Jesus Christ who is at His right hand, accompanying (as well as preceding and following) the creature, and, also, as ruling the creature, and the latter can be described in New Testament terms as the kingdom of God.[72] Barth insists that it is God and God alone who rules. "Proceeding from God and accompanied by God, the creature must return to God." In addition, "the glory of God is in the salvation and glorification of the creature.[73]

Barth then points to the five indicators of God's rule in world history. These are: the holy Scripture in its origin, transmission, and interpretation; the history of the Church, resulting from Scripture, and its capacity for resistance and renewal; the extraordinary identity and survival of the Jews in which our sin and God's electing grace can be viewed; and, fourthly and surprisingly, the limitation of human life universally and the once only place of personal history and opportunity to hear God's word. And, finally, Barth mentions the angels as a sign of God's rule in history, more important than the previous ones. [74]

Although Christians will find much that baffles and confuses them in worldly events, they know and trust the Lordship of God from within. The distinctive knowledge that they have is exemplified in the triple Christian attitude of faith, obedience, and prayer.[75]

Barth follows with section 50 on God and Nothingness, a section which has proved very controversial and should, therefore, be expounded fairly fully. This is the alien and opposing element from which God defends His own. In the German the original term is *Das Nichtige*, the Nihil, that which is ultimately *not*. This is overruled by God, but neither God nor the creature is the author of it, hence God neither wills nor permits it. In the Incarnation we learn from Christ that nothingness includes sin, but it is far more than sin, since it includes real sin, evil, death, and the devil.[76] In his own summaries of nothingness Barth makes four major points: first, it is "the adversary whom God has regarded, attacked and routed as His own enemy" and this will be generally revealed in the return of Jesus Christ.[77] Secondly, while it has no ultimate power and significance, yet "only a dangerous semblance of them are to be attributed to the existence, menace, corruption, disturbance, and destructiveness of nothingness as these may still be seen."[78] In the third place, it can only have its semblance of validity under God's decree.[79] Finally, in the form still left to it "nothingness exists and functions under the control of God, and we must say that even though it does not will to do so it is forced to serve Him, to serve His Word and work, the honor of His Son, the proclamation of the Gospel, the faith of the community, and therefore the way which He Himself wills to go within and with His creation until its day is done."[80]

Finally, in Volume III, part 3, Barth turns to consider the Kingdom of Heaven and God's ambassadors (the angels) and their opponents (the demons).[81] In the cosmos of heaven and earth, God is nearer heaven and so heaven is superior to earth, and this an invisible sphere bordering earth. God's will is done in heaven and it has earth as its aim. Angels are the entourage of God in heaven, and they function as His ambassadors, who do His will and act as His witnesses, and they confirm God's Word and work to creatures of the earth. They are, therefore, rightly considered a part of the Divine providence. Demons are the enemies of angels, whom they lyingly imitate. God's truth discovers their falsehood and Christ defeated them. As to any angelic fall, Barth rather cursorily objects to the verses that imply a fall of angels, but without supporting his viewpoint with any other directly related Scriptures. On this particular point Geoffrey Bromiley comments: "When he (Barth) has done so much to restore angels (and demons) as a theme of serious theological enquiry, it is a pity that the whole discussion should end with so questionable a thesis and procedure."[82]

5. A Critique of Barth's General Doctrine of Providence

Next we proceed to evaluate Barth's general theory of providence, which is also Christologically dominated. John Hick in his well-argued *Evil and the God of Love* has some trenchant criticisms of Barth. He is fair in expounding Barth's *Das Nichtige* as inimical to God, taking the form of sin and pain, suffering and death, and is at God's left hand, as the *opus alienum*, as grace at God's right hand is the *opus proprium*, and the destruction of nothingness and chaos will be revealed in the return of Christ in glory (the *parousia*). Hick finds three weaknesses in this conception of Barth's. In the first place, he thinks the appropriate word should be *Das Böse* (evil) for *Das Nichtige* (Nothingness of Chaos) and believes it a weakness that Barth should, in his general rejection of philosophy have revived an ancient, meontic tradition of Neo-Platonism, although its modern exponents have included theologians such as Berdyaev and atheistic existentialists such as Sartre and Heidegger.[83] This view has all the weaknesses of Augustine's conception of evil as absence of goodness considered in Chapter II.

Hick's second objection centers on the origin of *Das Nichtige* as recounted by Barth as an act of Divine rejection involved in the creation of a good universe, which he characterizes not only as sheer speculation, but also as "a naively mythological construction, which cannot stand rational criticism."[84] The real difficulty which Barth does not solve is this: "We are left in a strange position indeed! Evil (in the sense of *Das Nichtige* came to 'be' as that which God repudiated when He created the universe. But Barth does not feel obliged to suppose that it thus came to 'be' either by a necessity independent of the Divine will, or by the Divine will itself. He not only refuses to choose between these possibilities, but by implication he repudiates both!"[85] Hick further attacks Barth for his claim to find the basis of his theory in Genesis 1, which is "a quite patent imposing of his own speculation upon the text." [86]

Thirdly, Hick asks why Barth does not conceive that God was able, had He so wished, to create a good universe unaccompanied by the menacing shadow of rejected evil? Or, alternatively, Barth could have argued that God has deliberately created the conditions under which evil has arisen and permits its existence in the world for a good purpose. In that case, Hick wittily adds that if evil was a necessary pre-condition of the supreme good of redemption, "Thus instead of 'O felix culpa . . . ' we might sing 'O felix Nihil, quae talem ac tantum meruit habere redemptorem.'"[87] But Barth did not take this way out, presumably in order to free God from the imputation of responsibility for evil and because it would manifest a limitation of His freedom. But Barth's inconclusive alternative scheme limits the Divine power doubly, for as to *Das Nichtige*, "God can defeat it—at a great cost—but He cannot avoid having to defeat it. On either view God is ultimately defined as a limited God."[88] Hick concludes that the concept of non-being may have its use as poetic diction, but as an ontological or metaphysical concept it represents a mistaken hypostatization and even reification of language without help in relation to the problem of theodicy.[89]

After these trenchant criticisms, Hick concludes that there are constructive values in Barth's treatment of Nothingness. One is the distinction which he makes between the shadow side of creaturely existence (what is traditionally known as metaphysical evil), and evil in the more virulent sense of which the primary expression is sin. The second advantage is that Barth stresses in his vivid fashion that the evils of the shadow side have become deadly and inimical to God's purposes only in man because of his state of alienation from God.[90]

Charles Duthie, English theologian, offers other criticisms of Barth's exposition of general providence. His first charge reminds us that Barth suggests that contemporary theologians have an anxiety-complex over synergism in order to protect man's capacity to cooperate with God, in the words, "as though perhaps we were ascribing too much to God and too little to the creature . . . What sorry lip servants we are! And there is a reason for it. For the very depths of the Church, in the very depths of Christian conscience and Christian theology, our fear of God is in fact far stronger than the love with which we are able to love God."[91] Duthie retorts with a *tu quoque*. This is his counterblast to Barth's blast: "This is a passage which makes us ask . . . whether he himself has not such an anxiety-complex with regard to synergism [man cooperating with God] that he fails to do justice to the reality of the freedom of man."[92] Duthie and others have felt that for all Barth's emphasis on grace, he has described the relationship of God to man as dominating rather than persuasive, and that this is a necessary consequence of insisting on the denial of *liberum arbitrium* (a freewill which allows equal opportunity for choice).

But Barth's response to this criticism would be that evil is no real option for the Christian acting under the inspiration of the Holy Spirit and desiring the obedience of faith for which he was created by the loving Lord of history. Duthie judges: "What is needed to correct and amplify Barth's teaching is the reminder that once we have seen God in Jesus we know that this grace is not only condescending and undeserved, it is persuasive and accommodating. Because he is Love, God lays Himself alongside His world and the personal beings He has created. He seeks to win without dominating."[93] Duthie, too, finds the meontic argument about the role of nothingness unsatisfactory, and suggests it would be an improvement for Barth, "with de Chardin and other modern writers, to accept the universe as a universe in which evil arises through the processes of disorder and failure, of decay, of solitude and anxiety, and of growth itself. Evil comes to be precisely because our world is a world built for the development of freedom, the growth in wisdom and love of personal spirits." He concludes: "Barth is haunted by the fear of making God the author of evil! The Nihil might even be regarded as a device to avoid this possibility." [94]

Another important Dutch theologian in the Reformed tradition is Hendrik Berkhof. While he considers Barth's Christocentric concentration admirable, he finds him unsatisfactory in neglecting other themes such as "the work of the Holy Spirit, and particularly the Holy Spirit's relation to the realm of history."[95]

Geoffrey Wainwright offers an entirely different set of criticisms of Barth. He faults him for a general disinterest in liturgy and in visual art, asserting that Barth was locked into "the liturgical insipidity of German-speaking Switzerland" characterized by Wainwright as accepting a truncated liturgy without the Lord's Supper, as if Barth was pleased to accept an order of worship consisting of "a sermon surrounded by a couple of prayers and a couple of hymns." He does, however, give Barth credit, as one might expect a Methodist critic to do, for appreciating the theological importance of congregational singing. However, he also faults Barth thus: "He was gravely suspicious of the visual: the plastic arts are too 'static,' 'fixed'; whereas the congregation should be moving on from one provisional Amen to another, and even the best artists are 'necessarily' either docetic as in 'the great Italians', or ebionite, as in Rembrandt (C. D., IV, 867-68)." Thus Wainwright concludes, "the icon and with it the whole world of Eastern Orthodoxy were closed to him."[96]

Furthermore, since all of Providence and even of theodicy for Barth is Christologically controlled, we must consider Berkouwer's criticism of Barth's eschatology. Barth virtually denies the possibility of human life after death as an implicate of man's finite character. Yet, says Berkouwer, our later "no longer being in the definitive sense in which Barth posits it, is exactly what Scripture denies."[97]

J. B. Soucek, in an article published in 1949, pointed to the difficulty and apparent inadequacy of Barth's eschatology, with the question: "Is not the Christian hope too much narrowed down until it becomes a quite unimaginable moment of meeting with God, or an elevation of the mere finite past and not-to-be-continued existence of man into the light of God's grace, God's forgiveness and God's purpose?"[98] One must conclude that Barth's eschatology is an obscuring and a limitation of the New Testament's proclamation of the glory of eternal life. Consequently, Barth's denial of eternal life for humanity casts the longest and darkest shadow on his celebration of the joy that the grace of Christ brings. It calls for muffled drums, not for the sound of trumpets reflecting the everlasting light of God, and sounding forth His harmony.

In his brief, perceptive book, *Karl Barth Theologian* (1983) John Bowden has a chapter entitled "Problem" where he attempts an assessal of Barth both negative and positive. In his view Barth's weaknesses appear to be three. In the first place, Barth has not produced a satisfactory way of relating theology to other disciplines, and he quotes D. F. Ford to this effect: "The result is that, instead of offering a way of handling the manifold mutual interpenetration of theology, comparative religion, history, psychology, philosophy, and the natural sciences, his rigid boundaries simplify the picture by excluding much relevant material."[99] One is therefore bound to question his transcendent positivism of revelation, so Bowden writes in consequence: "Is alleged knowledge of God outside Jesus

Christ really *qualitatively* different in every instance from knowledge of God in Christ as Barth described it?"[100]

In the second place, Barth seems to have been far too disinterested in the historicity of the record of the life of Jesus, although this has been a major critical inquiry since the time of the publication of Schweitzer's *The Quest of the Historical Jesus* to the present day. Thirdly, Bowden asks, since Barth acknowledges that revelation and Scripture are not co-terminous, although an event happens through Scripture, can this view stand up to historical criticism?[101]

However, Bowden admires the man greatly, and the penetrating questions which he asked in the *Dogmatics* if he was not always able to answer them fully. Bowden also admires the joy of his spirit, and commits himself to the statement: "The remark that Barth's theology is perhaps still the single corpus most necessary to understanding twentieth-century theology is no exaggeration."[102] His final tribute is: "One comes to love Barth, warts and all, as one can love no other of the great twentieth-century theologians . . . "[103] As an encomium it falls far short of the eulogy of the English translators of Barth's *Dogmatics*, with their praise of "the great Church Father of Evangelical Christendom, the one genuine Doctor of the Universal Church the modern era has known," and they conclude: "Only Athanasius, Augustine, Aquinas and Calvin performed comparable service in the past, in the search for a unified and comprehensive basis for all theology in the grace of God."[104] Only the future can tell whether Barth should join such exalted company as an equal.

Whatever criticisms have been made of the developing theology of Barth, which have mainly concerned themselves with his 'incipient universalism'[105] and, as a consequence, the possible lack of incentives for sanctification and mission and the already assured victory of God in the Incarnation. Other criticisms have included the lack of freedom in the understanding of faith, as well as the difficulties caused by the concept of *Das Nichtige* and the obscurity in his combination of terminality and yet eternalizing of men in his eschatology, and his substitution of eristics for apologetics, and his frequently harsh treatment of theologians who differed from him,[106] these are dark spots on the sun.

6. Barth's Great Gifts as Theologian and Man

Against these must be weighed in the scale the persistent, careful, responsible, consistent Christocentric concentration throughout; the detailed exegeses with which his theses are supported, the attractive and brilliant architectonic of the treatment; the cultural references to music (especially Mozart) and to painting (Botticelli and Grünewald), to literature and to philosophy; the extraordinary knowledge of the Fathers in East and West, the Scholastics of the Middle Ages, the Reformers, and the modern theologians (especially those of the nineteenth century); the courage of the man who backed the Confessing Church in its struggle with the Nazis and the same courage in seeking forgiveness instead of vengeance for the defeated Germans from the Allies, and the courage to see that democracy had an economic as well as a political basis which was forgotten by the virulent anti-Communists. All this is part of the many-sided life of Barth, the pastor, the university professor, the prophet, the preacher to the prisoners, the social democrat, the lover of music and player of the viola,[107] admirer of circuses, the reader of detective stories, the raconteur, and the wit.

His greatest achievement is, of course, the work of almost forty years—*Kirchliche Dogmatik*—which, in its original white binding was affectionately called in Germany "the great white whale" in its thirteen volumes, over nine thousand pages and six million words, making it nine times as long as Calvin's *Institutes.*[108] It took four decades of hard, painstaking, reflective labor. Barth will live because of this great unfinished *magnum opus*, in which he tried to resist the secularizing tendencies of faith in our times with indefatigable energy and perceptiveness, as the American novelist, John Updike, recently acknowledged.[109]

What Barth's sources were other than the Scriptures, can be discovered easily from the books he kept by him in the smaller study in the smaller house to which he moved on a hill above Basle in 1955. Here, too, was Grünewald's Crucifixion that demonstrated both the self-emptying of the eternal Son of God and the costliness of human redemption in stark realism. Christ's brow is lacerated by the crown of thorns, the eyes are haggard, the tongue is desiccated, the fingers are splayed and stiff, the sagging body is pockmarked and pustular where the wounds do not gape, and the feet and arms are contorted. On the left of the Cross St. John supports the mourning Virgin Mother, while Mary Magdalene kneels with suppliant crossed hands, not caring where her long golden tresses fall, and to her side is the flask of ointment she has brought. On the right near the foot of the Cross is a live lamb with a chalice and a miniature cross, symbolizing "the Lamb slain from the foundation of the world" (Romans 13:8) and the benefits of Holy Communion, while dominating above it is the austere figure of John the Baptist, as Witness to the Messiah, with his elongated index figure pointing to the Crucified Lord,[110] saying, "He must increase, but I must decrease." (John 3:30).

The choice of this painting as a focus was a perpetual reminder to Barth of his duty to expound a thoroughly Christ-centered theology. That duty he fulfilled in exemplary fashion, as three final tributes will attest. The first is by Bela Vassady, a Hungarian theologian living in Communist-dominated Eastern Europe, who affirms that he learned much from Barth, and especially from his Christ-centered doctrine of providence: "To interpret Divine providence only in the context of God's gracious election. Once we learned that the greatest crime committed in human history (Jesus' crucifixion) did not take God by surprise and that it was used for our salvation, we shall have no difficulty in interpreting the tragic events in our own lives, in the life of our nation, and even in the life of the whole globe from the perspective of God's purposeful providence." [111]

Robert McAfee Brown honors most of all Barth's reinterpretation of predestination as utterly good news, as well as his combination of neo-orthodoxy with the radical social implications of the Gospel: "And as I reflect on the baleful influence on the church and on the human *psyche* of centuries of Augustian-Thomistic-Calvinistic predestination, I am grateful that the shroud has been lifted by Barth and the human endeavor can again be affirmed as an endeavor blessed, rather than cursed, by God." On the second point he adds: "As Barth puts it, in words that might just so easily be found in Gutierrez [leading liberation theologian]: 'God always takes His stand unconditionally and passionately on this side and on this side alone: Against the lofty and on behalf of the lowly, against those who already enjoy right and privilege and on behalf of those who are denied it and deprived of it.' (C. D. II, 1. 386)."[112]

Our third and final testimony to Barth comes from Langdon Gilkey, like Robert McAfee Brown, an American theologian who finds in Barth originality, immense courage, realism about religion, "a radar set for the realities of our epoch," a universalistic theology, and, most compelling of all, the impression that "No one has ever had a more thorough and irresistible (unarguable-against) apprehension of the priority of God, of God's actions, and so of revelation and grace in all sound theology."[113]

Despite the four centuries that divide Barth from Calvin, there is a basic unity between them and that is to be found in the following citation from the *Institutes*: "Christ is the mirror wherein we must, and without self-deception may, contemplate our own election."[114]

Notes

1 Book VIII, 12.

2 The change in Barth is described by him thus. "For me personally a day in the beginning of August in that year (1914) was the *dies ater* [the black day], when ninety-three German intellectuals published an endorsement of the military policy of Kaiser Wilhelm II and his councillors, on which to my horror I found the names of almost all the theological teachers whom hitherto I had confidently respected. If they could be so mistaken in ethos, I noted that it was quite impossible for me to adhere any longer to their ethics or dogmatics, to their exposition of the Bible or presentation of history. So far as I was concerned there was no more future for the theology of the nineteenth century." Quoted in ed. E. J. Tinsley, *Modern Theology, Volume 1: Karl Barth, 1886-1968* (London: Epworth Press, 1973), p. 37. See also Eberhard Busch, *Karl Barth, His life from letters and autobiographical texts* (Philadelphia: Fortress Press, 1976), pp. 80 ff.

3 Busch, *op. cit.*, pp. 245-248.

4 *Church Dogmatics* (afterwards abbreviated to C. D.) II, 1, p. 458.

5 For example, the *Dogmatics* has extensive citations from early medieval, reformed, and modern theologians, as well as many extended references to such philosophers as Aristotle, Plato, Plotinus, Spinoza, Kant, Hegel, Kierkegaard, Nietzsche, Heidegger and Sartre, not forgetting literary giants such as Milton, Goethe, Ibsen and Dostoievsky, and several important historians. Also, see Paul Lehmann's account of Barth's library in ed. Donald McKim, *How Karl Barth Changed My Mind* (Grand Rapids, Michigan: Eerdmans, 1986), p. 38.

6 C. D., I, 2, p. 506.

7 C. D., I, 2, p. 507.

8 C. D., I, 2, p. 512.

9 C. D., I, 2, pp. 512-513.

10 C. D., I, 2, p. 513.

11 C. D., I, 2, p. 514.

12 C. D., I, 2, p. 537.

13 C. D., I, 1, pp. 98ff.

14 *The Theology of Karl Barth: An Introduction* (Philadelphia: The Westminster Press, 1965), p. 61. The sections of the *Church Dogmatics* referred to are II, 1, pp. 172 ff. and IV, 3, p. 3.

15 *Op. cit.*, p. 15.

16 C. D., II, 1, p. 351: "We must recognize and understand all His perfections as the perfections of His love. This is in spite of the fact that at first glance we might suppose that we ought to seek the divinity of the divine being much rather in the freedom of God, *i.e.*, in His unity, constancy and eternity, in His omnipresence, omnipotence and glory." But Barth stresses love first and recognizes freedom and its consequent attributes second, because of the primacy of Christ's revelation of God as love.

17 C. D., II, 2, p. ix.

18 C. D., II, 2, p. 3; also C. D., II, 2, p. 34.

19 C. D., II, 2, p. 13.

20 Ibid. For the Weber source, see *The Protestant Ethic and the Spirit of Capitalism* (New York: Scribners, ca. 1958), pp. 101, 104.

21 C. D., II, 2, p. 39. The Calvin reference is to the *Institutes* III, xxiv, 12.

22 C. D., II, 2, pp. 37 ff. The Otten reference is to *Calvins theologische Anschauung von der Praedestination* (Munich: Chr. Kaiser, 1939), p. 34.

23 C. D., II, 2, pp. 36-44 ff.

24 C. D., II, 2, pp. 58 ff. "It is God's choice that under the name of Jesus Christ He wills to give life to the substance of His people's history and to that people itself, constituting Himself its Lord and Shepherd." (p. 54)

25 C. D., II, 2, p. 103.

26 C. D., II, 2, p. 105. On p. 111 Barth says: "the electing God of Calvin is a *deus nudus absconditus* . . . All the dubious features of Calvin's doctrine result from the basic failing that in the last analysis he separates God and Jesus Christ, thinking that what was in the beginning with God must be sought elsewhere than in Jesus Christ."

27 C. D., II, 2, pp. 120-127.

28 C. D., II, 2, p. 143.

29 C. D., II, 2, p. 161.

30 C. D., II, 2. p. 167.

31 C. D., II, 2, p. 194.

32 C. D., II, 2, p. 201.

33 C. D., II, 2, p. 210.

34 C. D., II, 2, pp. 211 ff.

35 C. D., II, 2, pp. 315 ff.

36 C. D., II, 2, pp. 345-349.

37 C. D., II, 2, pp. 417 ff. Barth concludes this passage by asserting: "But, again, in grateful recognition of the grace of divine freedom we cannot venture the opposite statement that there cannot and will not be this final opening up and enlargement of the circle of election and calling." (p. 419)

38 C. D., II, 2, p. 345.

39 C. D., II, 2, p. 415.

40 C. D., II, 2, pp. 449-450.

41 C. D., II, 2, pp. 455 ff.

42 C. D., II, 2, pp. 459-571.

43 *Introduction to the Theology of Karl Barth* (Grand Rapids: Eerdmans, ca. 1979), p. 97.

44 C. D., II, 2, p. 506.

45 *The Christian Doctrine of God*, Chapter 22, gives Brunner's exposition of "The Eternal Divine Decrees and the Doctrine of Election." His insistence upon combining the holiness and mercy of God appears on p. 337.

46 *Op. cit.*, pp. 314-315.

47 *Op. cit.*, p. 335.

48 *The Theology of Karl Barth.* An Introduction (Philadelphia: Westminster Press, 1965), p. 187.

49 *Historic Protestantism and Predestination* (Philadelphia: The Presbyterian and Reformed Publishing Company, n.d.), p. 103.

50 *Introduction to the Theology of Karl Barth*, p. 96.

51 *Op. cit.*, p. 97.

52 *Op. cit.*, pp. 97-98.

53 *The Significance of Barth's Theology: An Appraisal with Special Reference to Election and Reconciliation* (Grand Rapids: Baker Book House, 1961), p. 70.

54 *Op. cit.*, p. 71.

55 *Ibid.*

56 To give only one example, see W. J. Hausmann, *Karl Barth's Doctrine of Election* (New York: Philosophical Library, 1969), who writes: "There will be greater enthusiasm in preaching the Gospel of Jesus Christ—greater emphasis on what Christ has done for us rather than what we have to do. One will preach on the defeat of sin as the primary emphasis rather than on sin as a reality, on eternal salvation as a primary emphasis rather than on eternal damnation." (pp. 88-89) See *passim* ed. D. McKim, *How Karl Barth Changed My Mind*, and esp. pp. 27-78.

57 Barth made this charge in C. D., II, 2, p. 118.

58 Berkouwer, *The Triumph of Grace* . . . , p. 286, cites the following sentence of Calvin to make his point: "But if we have been chosen in Him [Christ] we shall not find assurance of our election in ourselves; and not even in God the Father, if we conceive Him as severed from His Son." (*Institutes*, III, 24, 5.) Berkouwer provides the Latin original of the conditional final phrase of the citation: *Ac ne in Deo quidem Patri, si nudum illum absque Filio imaginamur.*

59 This occurs in C. D., IV, 1, p. 454, and Berkouwer comments on it both on pp. 61-2 and pp. 231-247.

60 *Op. cit.*, p. 258.

61 Op. cit., pp. 231 and 233.

62 Brunner's *The Christian Doctrine of God*, p. 379.

63 *Op. cit.*, p. 237.

64 *Op. cit.*, p. 270.

65 *Op. cit.*, p. 299.

66 *Ibid.*

67 C. D., IV, 1, p. 271.

68 *Op. cit.*, p. 304.

69 *Ibid.*

70 *Op. cit.*, pp. 314, 316.

71 This is a summary of Section 48 and the beginning of Section 49.

72 A summary of C. D., III, 3, pp. 58-157.

73 A summary of C. D., III, 3, pp. 158-159.

74 A summary of C. D., III, 3, pp. 187-243.

75 A summary of C. D., III, 3, pp. 244-248.

76 A summary of C. D., III, 3, pp. 289-310. See the editorial note on the translation of *Das Nichtige* in C. D., III, 3, p. 289.

77 C. D., III, 3, p. 366.

78 C. D., III, 3, p. 367.

79 *Ibid.*

80 *Ibid.*

81 C. D., III, 3, Section 51.

82 *Introduction to the Theology of Karl Barth* (Grand Rapids: Eerdmans, 1989), p. 155. I have found Bromley's book invariably accurate, concise, clear, comprehensive, and sympathetic as a summary of the massive volumes of Barth's *Church Dogmatics*, with occasional pertinent criticisms.

83 John Hick, *Evil and the God of Love* (New York: Harper & Row, 1961), p. 141. This meontic philosophy which Augustine derived from Neo-Platism, found a new life in Nicholas Berdyaev, *The Destiny of Man*, Paul Tillich's *Systematic Theology*, I and II (who calls it "Non-being"), while Sartre names it "le néant", and Heidegger "das Nichts".

84 *Op. cit.*, p. 141.

85 *Op. cit.*, p. 149.

86 *Ibid.*

87 *Op. cit.*, p. 145.

88 *Ibid.*

89 *Op. cit.*, p. 193.

90 *Op. cit.*, p. 150.

91 C. D., III, 3, 196.

92 Ed. Maurice Wiles, *Providence* (London: S.P.C.K., 1969), chapter 5 by Charles Duthie, p. 68.

93 *Op. cit.*, p. 76.

94 *Op. cit.*, pp. 74-75.

95 Ed. Donald M. McKin, *How Karl Barth Changed My Life* (Grand Rapids: Wm. E. Eerdmans Publishing Company, 1986), p. 21.

96 *Ibid.*, p. 180.

97 C. D. III, 2, p. 271. Barth also speaks in his Ethics of the once-for-all opportunity, thus underlining the terminal nature of finite human life as judgment, in C. D. III, 4, Section 56, and this is also mentioned in II, 3, pp. 70-73 and occasionally referred to in III, 4, pp. 653-682.

98 "Man in the light of the Humanity of Jesus", The *Scottish Journal of Theology*, March 1949, p. 81. This is a very fair attempt to understand Barth's view which emphasizes the "eternalizing" of our finite life as contrasted with any kind of continuity in eternity. Yet the Very Reverent Dr. Thomas F. Torrance assured me (October 11, 1989) that in his last interview with Barth, the latter asserted his firm belief in the resurrection of the body.

99 "Conclusion: Assessing Barth", in ed. S. W. Sykes, *Karl Barth: Studies of His Theological Method* (Oxford: Clarendon Press, 1989), p. 194, cited J. Bowden, *op. cit.*, p. 114.

100 Bowden, *Karl Barth Theologian* (London, S.C.M. Press, 1983), p. 96.

101 *Op. cit.*, p. 99.

102 *Op. cit.*, p. 101.

103 *Ibid.*

104 C. D. IV, 4, p. vi.

105 See the important article of Joseph D. Bettis, "Is Karl Barth a Universalist?", *The Scottish Journal of Theology*, vol. XX, pp. 423-436, to which the answer is "No.".

106 John Cobb maintains that Barth harshly and unfairly accused both Brunner and Niebuhr of accepting the values of natural theology as if they were thereby guilty of undervaluing revelation and supernatural theology. This is *odium theologicum*. Hence Cobb asserts: "There was no need for him to misrepresent such colleagues as Emil Brunner and

Reinhold Niebuhr and attack them so brutally." (Ed. D. M. McKim, *op. cit.*, p. 172).

107 One recalls his famous remark: "Whether the angels play only Bach in praising God I am not quite sure; I am sure, however, that *en famille* they play Mozart, and then also God the Lord is especially delighted to listen to them." From Walter Leibrecht (ed.), *Religion and Culture: Essays in Honor of Paul Tillich* (London: S.C.M. Press, 1959), p. 64.

108 Eberhard Busch, *Karl Barth. His Life from letters and autobiographical texts*, trans. John Bowden (London: S.C.M. Press, 1976), p. 486.

109 In *Self-Consciousness, Memoirs* (New York: Alfred A. Knopf, 1989), p. 149: "I had learned from Kierkegaard and Barth to say the worst about our earthly condition, which was hopeless without a scandalous supernatural redemption . . . "

110 *Op. cit.*, p. 116. Barth refers to this picture thus: "John the Baptist with his hand pointing in an almost impossible way. It is this hand which is in evidence in the Bible."

111 Ed. McKim, *Ibid.*, p. 33.

112 *Ibid.*, p. 99.

113 *Ibid.*, pp. 153-54.

114 IV. 24, 5.

Chapter 6

Conclusion

This book was limited to an exposition and critique of the doctrine of providence in Western theology. If it had included Eastern theology, we would certainly have considered the theology of providence in the exposition of St. John Chrysostom, possibly the greatest preacher in the history of Christianity, both for the fidelity of his Biblical hermeneutics, Antiochene rather than Alexandrian and allegorical in character,[1] and because he wrote an admirable treatise on providence. Our scope, however, was broad enough in dealing with two Catholic and two Protestant theologians in Western Christianity during a period of fifteen hundred years.

The two Protestant theologians, Calvin and Barth, dealt more faithfully with the Biblical exposition of the doctrine than the Catholic theologians, because the latter were primarily philosophical rather than kerygmatic theologians, and brilliantly so in the case of both Saint Augustine and Saint Thomas Aquinas, with the former using Plato and Plotinus as his apologetical ally, and the second turning Aristotle from an enemy to a friend of the faith.

We must inquire of the four theologians whom we studied in some detail two questions. The first is: Are the attributes of God as you conceive them closer to Aristotle's Unmoved Mover and First Cause than to the holy and merciful God of the Old and New Testaments in Whom love is greater than absolute power? The second is: How have you dealt with the problem of correlating Divine omnipotence and human freedom?

* * *

God in Augustine's thinking is clearly impassible; that is, in His perfections incapable of the weakness of suffering. As omnipotent He is the source of all goodness and grace and power. The result is that human beings have no free will. This is because all are slaves to evil through the damnable heritage of original sin and original guilt inherited through Adam's disobedience. This can only be overcome by the irresistibility of God's grace, for the weakened will cannot obey God apart from grace. The key Biblical passage for Augustine is Romans 5:12: ἐφ' ᾧ πάντεζ ἥμαρτον. Furthermore, although they *must* sin, through the concept of seminal identity they are held responsible for the sins of their ancestors, which is morally unacceptable to most modern theologians. Nor does Augustine do justice to God by declaring His will inscrutable, instead of seeing that he is presenting an unjust God who acts towards the predeterminedly reprobate—the vast majority of His creation—as a capricious tyrant reducing humans to the status of puppets or robots.

Nor can we accept Augustine's view that traces all the evil in the world as due to sin or to the punishment of sin, since both the Book of Job and the witness of Christ in Luke 13:1-5 and John 9:1-5 reject such a view outright. His mistake—and not only his—was to consider the nature and activity of God in terms of substance and power rather than in personal categories. But Augustine's sense of the grace of God in the undeserved redemption of the elect was admirable.

* * *

We see in Saint Thomas Aquinas a brilliantly and rigorously analytical theology, a philosophical theology. No other theologian has had so firm a conviction of the value of human reason as a propaedutic or preparation for the acceptance of Divine revelation, both of them gifts of the same Triune God. In his five arguments for the existence of God, as in his finely organized and well argued *Summae*, he consistently contends for the coordination of human reason and Divine revelation, while, of course, claiming supremacy for revelation over reason when received by faith. He also affirms the supremacy of the apophatic or negative theology since God transcends human knowledge, and he further insists on the supremacy of the ultimate knowledge of God in eternity through the unveiled vision of God.

In the area of Providence, while greatly dependent upon the teaching of Augustine, St. Thomas does remove some of the gravamen of the charge that God was unjust and that the elect are the favorites of God, by maintaining that although the reprobates cannot obtain grace, yet their falling into sin continually comes from their abuse of free will. Still, although the elect despite undeserving have been granted some degree of grace, some degree of unfairness can still be imputed to God. There is also a basic difference in conception of God held respectively by Augustine and Aquinas. God, for Augustine, was unchanging, strictly immutable. For Aquinas God is conceived more dynamically as the pure act of Being (*actus purus*).

Aquinas also treats of the three traditional aspects of Providence: Creation, Preservation, and Government, but his delight and wonder is in the effectiveness of God's *gubernatio*, which provides the entire order of the universe in space and time. He is equally concerned to maintain the Divine control of events (although Augustine's *City of God* was a much more imaginative conception of God's control of history) along with the genuineness of human freedom of choice. Here he follows the earlier Augustine who later came to negate free will by insistence on the slavery of the will, thus intending to maintain the absolute sovereignty of God. So, while double predestination is not emphasized as in Augustine, yet St. Thomas Aquinas cites Titus 3:5 and Romans 9:11-12 as contradicting any view that the elect are those whose obedience to His will God foresees (a view put forward by Origen of Alexandria). This view of Aquinas does not guarantee God's mercy (far from it!), but it supposedly emphasizes the generosity of God in the salvation of the undeserving elect. Finally, and unsatisfactorily to most modern theologians, the choice to save or damn is attributed to the inscrutability of the Divine will.

However, it must be recognized that St. Thomas acknowledges free will as an effect of God's love seen in the elect, so that God then receives spontaneous human responses to His love.

Even when Aquinas affirms, with St. Augustine, that evil is absence of good, and that it is in inferior beings in which this lack is seen, which denies the sinister and damaging effects of evil in the world, he does produce an ingenious new argument. This is to the effect that the justice needed in the universe requires that sinners should receive penalties, hence God is the source of evil as penalty, but not of evil as fault.

Finally, St. Thomas Aquinas recognizes that the Divine Providence reaches as far as eternity where it is expressed in the blessedness of the vision of God and the total triumph of Grace.

* * *

Calvin is clearly a Biblical rather than a philosophical theologian, and this provides his strength as well as some of his apologetical difficulties. He sees in human success (that is, in righteous not infamous success) the blessing of God and in human adversity the curse of God. The result is that human unhappiness is explicable and bearable either as punishment for sin, or a test of patience, or an incitation for self-denial for the faithful. Ultimately, it is regarded for the Christian as an entering into the fellowship of Christ's sufferings which is the ultimate justification for and sanctification of suffering by which men and women learn the obedience of faith. These convictions had a tonic effect on those who believed themselves to belong to the elect. It was, however, counter-productive, for any who were unsure whether they were elect or reprobate, as in the case of the seventeenth century Puritans in North America.[2] This is because there were two sources of ambiguity: the dualism which attributed the cause of dark events to the Devil or to the anger of God, and belief that the elect were very few and the reprobate very many. Calvin also reiterated Augustine's conviction that God can make good issue out of evil, as in the cases of Joseph sold into slavery by his brothers who ultimately saves them and their father, and supremely Jesus in Gethsemane in turning the miscarriage of justice in the Crucifixion into the means of human salvation.

Furthermore, Calvin argues that the ultimate justification of the Divine benevolence is eschatological—it will be known in eternity—and is now to be accepted by the heirs of hope in faith.

Difficulties arise in the development of the doctrine of Predestination. Calvin sees its value in the insistence that Election safeguards salvation as wholly the gift of God, which is neither won nor deserved by humans, and he further insists that this safeguards humility as well as creating confidence in believers amidst struggles and mortal dangers. Granted all these advantages, nonetheless predestination is a hidden decree and in Calvin's own description it is a *decretum horribile*, a frightening or terrifying decree.

The criticisms of double Predestination that seem valid are, however much Biblical evidence can be found for them in Paul's epistles (but not in the teaching of Jesus), and whatever the practical advantages of them to the elect, still the capricious tyranny of God, the favoritism for the elect and the injustice to the reprobates. Furthermore how can one hold men responsible for their sins if they have no freedom? The result is that for all Calvin's insistence upon the benevolence of God in nature, in human nature, and in the choice of the elect, the sovereign deterministic Deity resembles Aristotle's Unmoved Mover more than the God of Christ's greatest parable Who as a Father rushes out to meet the returning prodigal son and celebrates his home-coming with a feast.

And Calvin sees clearly the compassionate, forgiving, renewing, redemptive, and providential love of God, *but only chiefly for the elect.* It is this limitation which is unacceptable to many modern theologians. One is bound to wonder whether life was so difficult for Calvin in Geneva and if this led him to a Christian Stoicism which lacked a widespread sense of compassion for those who differed from him, so that God's sovereignty and justice for him overshadowed the patience and sacrificial compassion of the love of God revealed in Christ for the least and the lost.

But Calvin's theology and vertebral organization of the Church as well as the University of Geneva created courage, even if for the discouraged and doubtful it may have seemed like whistling in the dark. But, in fairness to Calvin, it should be remembered that he emphasized that God would grant perseverance to His elect.

Among Calvin's greatest strengths, however, it should be recalled, were obedience to the guidance of God's Word, and his profound pastoral recognition that the positive and negative directions of God's Providence build up the confidence of the faithful in the conviction that what Christ promises here and now He will make good here and hereafter.

* * *

The immense relief that Barth's reconsideration of Predestination brings is almost entirely due to the removal of the notion of the tyranny or the injustice of God. This is done by stressing the remarkable compassion of Christ, who becomes, in the Incarnation and in the Crucifixion the only reprobate that potentially all may become elect. No one has demonstrated the mightiness of Grace more dramatically or compassionately than Barth. He enables us to see God as love and freedom, and these emphases were masked in his predecessors by a dominant stress on the Divine Sovereignty.

Barth's own words are the following: "the doctrine of election is the sum of the Gospel because of all words that can be said or heard it is the best: that God elects man; that God is for man too the One who loves in freedom. It is grounded in Jesus Christ because He is both the electing God and elected man in one."[3] Five solid reasons are provided by Barth for discounting the doctrine as interpreted by Augustine, Aquinas and Calvin. First the traditional doctrine was far too negative. Next, it was based on a threat, not on the truth. Thirdly, it was an experience beginning with man, not with God, but it was fathered on God. Fourthly, its sovereign God was an abstraction in eternity, not the electing God in Christ. Finally, the doctrine was too individualistic, disregarding both of the communities of the Old and New Israel.

Furthermore, while insisting rightly on God's freedom, Barth allows a qualified degree of human freedom in permitting the elect almost infinite time in a given life before acknowledging their election. Moreover, he sees positive functions for the reprobates to fulfill: to represent the person who needs the Gospel, to show what is negated and overcome in the Gospel, and to give a man without a future a future in the Gospel.

In addition, Barth sees God's rule in human history in the ultimate establishment of the Kingdom of God. Whatever criticisms individuals have offered of particular parts of his systematic theology, there is almost universal agreement that he has valiantly attempted to counter the strong secularizing impact of the century with a theology that is Biblical, reassuring and relevant, combining Neo-orthodoxy with social justice.

* * *

But, what of the future interpretation of the doctrine of Providence? Future theologians, so one imagines, will not be able to go back on Barth's emphasis on God's 'Yes' rather than the 'No' of the traditional doctrine of the past. But also there will have to be no evasion of difficulties by making the Divine transcendence and its inevitable mystery an excuse for evading difficulties. Certainly there is a necessary recognition that our God, though a *Deus revelatus* in Christ can often seem in the dysteleological events in personal, family, or national life a hidden God, a *Deus absconditus*. This is the term that Pascal borrowed from the prophet Isaiah and in which he insisted that "There is enough light to lighten the elect, and enough darkness to humble them."[4]

Furthermore, an adequate doctrine of Providence for the twenty-first century must make full room for human freedom together with the Divine direction: the former has been emphasized by Process theologians, but unfortunately with a consequent loss of the Divine direction. This essential concurrence and concomitance is not easily defined.

Moreover, traditional theodicies described a deterministic, omnipotent, immutable, impassible Deity, conceived in Aristotelian terms of force or power. These characteristics have to be redefined so as to adequately express more convincingly the Judeo-Christian conception of the personal God in terms of compassion, love, forgiveness, holiness and grace.

In addition, because new knowledge (whether derived from scientific probes of the universe or from positive results of Biblical criticism) make some of the ancient formulations of Creation and Providence untenable, there must be revision, so that Faith and Reason may harmonize.

Finally, whatever residue of mystery remains in any account of Divine Providence, it cannot avoid, nor should it, the refulgence of light in darkness, which the mighty acts of God in the Incarnation, the Crucifixion and the Resurrection of Christ sheds in our darkness in the most agonizing of human experiences. In the interim, in these days of our confusion, Fideism may have to make do while we seek fuller metaphysical attempts to correlate the omnipotence, benevolence and goodness of God with the bitter realities of evil that exist in this world.

Notes

1 Of the six volumes of his writings translated in the Nicene and Post-Nicene Fathers, five are homilies expounding the Gospels and the Epistles.

2 See my *The worship of the American Puritans, 1629-1730* (New York: Peter Lang, 1990) chs. II and XII.

3 *Church Dogmatics*, II, 2, p. 3.

4 *Pensées*, No. 578.